LESSONS LEARNED

from the

Holy Spirit

My walk with the Holy Spirit and what I learned along the way.

Patrick Hackett-Kemp

Copyright © 2019 Patrick Hackett-Kemp

All rights reserved including the right to reproduce any part of this book without written permissions from the publisher, except by a reviewer who may quote brief passages or reproduce illustrations in a review with appropriate credits. Neither may any part of this book be reproduced, stored in a retrieval system, or transmitted in any form or by any means - electronic, mechanical, photocopying, recording, or other - without written permission from the publisher. For more information contact WALK ON NATIONS PUBLICATIONS. The information in this book is true and complete to the best of our knowledge. The author and the publisher disclaim any liability regarding the use of this information. WALK ON NATIONS PUBLICATIONS' books and media are available for special premium and promotional uses and for customized editions. WALK ON NATIONS PUBLICATIONS can bring Author Patrick Hackett Kemp and other speakers to your live event. For further information, please call 817-353-5114..

ISBN: 978-1-948290-05-0

CONTENTS

	Acknowledgments	i
	Introduction	v
1	What Do You Know About The Holy Spirit?	1
2	The Holy Spirit Has A History	9
3	The Holy Spirit Helps With Conversion	13
4	Lessons Learned Along The Way	18
5	Correct Understanding Of The Holy Spirit	23
6	The Holy Spirit Is Willing To Teach You	27
7	The Spirit Will Provide Direction	32
8	The Holy Spirit Reveals His Will For Your Life	40
9	A Lesson In Being Led By The Spirit	46
10	The Holy Spirit Will Guide Your Steps	52
11	Positioning Yourself To Hear The Holy Spirit	58
12	The Holy Spirit Speaks By Giving Impressions	67
13	Prompts From The Holy Spirit	75
14	How The Holy Spirit Gives Inner Conviction	81
15	The Holy Spirit And Supernatural Events	88
16	Be Willing To Be Led By The Spirit	95

17	The Holy Spirit Doesn't Shout, He Simply Whispers	99
18	The Holy Spirit Allows Us To Walk In The Supernatural	104
19	The Spirit Gives Us Revelation	108
20	Developing A Relationship With The Holy Spirit	118
	Conclusion	127
	About The Author	129

ACKNOWLEDGMENTS

To the Holy Spirit – I look forward to the journey ahead.

Kayla – to a woman that has pushed me toward greatness in her own unique way. May the adventure be prosperous and exciting along the way.

Camille, Taiylor, Gavin, Landon, Zion, and Xavier – your father is in the process of building a legacy in spite of distance and your youth. In time, you will see.

Gwenesta Price – proud to say you are my grandmother and the wisest among them all.

Cheryl Hackett – this book is a by-product of the summer before my fifth-grade year. I shall never forget, how you forced me to write a book report on the Ivory Coast, when the other kids where outside having fun. Your sacrifices and labor have not been in vain.

Larry & Reggie Kemp – the latter days have been produced support, a reflection of sacrifice, and the much-needed lessons of life as I navigate the unpredictable waters of manhood.

Lynne, Belinda (Washington), and Stevie Hackett – quitting has never been an option for this clan of siblings.

Your example gave me the proof that you must be willing to endure and tackle life challenges head on.

Uncle Charles Washington – you are probably sitting in the garage communicating with God in your own unique way or listening to Tupac Shakur (1 Chronicles 27:32)

Kenneth Franklin and Chaplain Robert Morris – our friendship has been tested by time, distance, common struggle, and loyalty along the way.

Pastor Rodney McIntosh – your spiritual support and integrity as a pastor has held me accountable, even during my most trying times. You believed in the gift, even at my lowest peaks.

Tre London – brotherhood has been bonded by our dreams for a better life and another way.

Eric Hill – your endurance in the midst of hardship and pain has been a constant reminder of your strength.

Michael Meadows – your keen insight is prophetic and reminds me of the sons of Issachar.

Pastor Brown and The Spoken Word Church – the gifts developed among this setting.

Pastor B.R. Daniels Sr. and the Beth Eden Baptist Church

Pastor James Womack - integrity and keen sense of discernment.

Ms. Cody – thank you for the book cover.

Ms. (Madea) 1 Kemp – the legacy shall continue on……

Patience and Howard Rose – the wisdom of guidance and experience helped make this dream a reality.

INTRODUCTION

It was just a normal blistering cold Sunday afternoon, in the easygoing city of Ogden, Utah when I made a quick run to the local Family Dollar by Weber State University after church. There I stood in the middle of the store when the Lord unexpectedly spoke to me about writing books. I picked up a copy of the Bible and the pages landed on Jeremiah 30:2, "This is what the Lord, the God of Israel, says: "Write in a book all the words I have spoken to you." It was just a few months after my relocation to Utah in the summer of 2007 and I was facing a very critical turning point in my life, to say least. I was smiling on the outside but inside I was suffering silently. And it seemed highly unlikely that while I was walking through the early stages of a divorce, God would be speaking to me about, among all things, writing books.

I sensed that He wanted to me begin chronicling my experiences to be published in books at one of the most trying times of my personal life. Expecting my third child, I had just been fired from my job before moving to Utah and I had less than a hundred dollars in cash, a few clothes, and books to add to the sum total of my earthly possessions. At certain times in my life, what little possessions I did have, found themselves in the hands of the local pawn shop clerks providing for my bare necessities to just make ends meet in my modest apartment. So trust me when I say, I didn't know at the time what God wanted me to write about at all. My personal failure as a young man and minister of the Gospel? Maybe...

A typical run one Sunday evening into the Family Dollar store in Ogden resulted in a prophetic moment that would shift my focus and mindset forever. That was over a decade ago! Looking back, I don't ever recall even once harboring the desire to write books, even though I'm an avid reader of literature. I figured that in the course of time, the Lord would reveal to me the topics and issues He would want me to write about as long as I continued seeking Him in prayer. And then it happened… In due time, while in prayer alone at the church one afternoon, I heard the Spirit of God say, "Lessons Learned From the Holy Spirit."

Meditating over matters that the Lord was dealing

with me about at the time, it was becoming quite obvious that many people (including me) in the Body of Christ were not living up to their full spiritual potential. How could this be I often wondered, when the scriptures possessed so many promises for His believers?

Years ago, a few weeks before preparing for a family vacation to Disney World, the Lord began to deal with me constantly about studying Him in the personality of the Holy Spirit. In my heart, I felt as if the Lord was revealing something to me that was missing in my walk with Him that would prove helpful down the road. Overnight, my spiritual interest and fascination with the Holy Spirit grew tremendously. The more study and research that was put in during the late-night hours while my family lay sound asleep proved to me to that my earlier inclinations were correct. I was suddenly aware that I and those around me who knew God, knew far less about Him in the form of the Holy Spirit than we should. Flipping through the pages of my personal library, researching on the internet, reading the Bible, and flipping through the pages of books in the library proved to be a valuable search. It was immediately obvious that I was not as knowledgeable about the Spirit of God as I should have been.

Growing up in my early days as a youth attending

church, Wednesday night Bible classes, or even at home, not once did I hear anyone talk about the importance of cultivating and maintaining a personal relationship with the Holy Spirit. It was beginning to become very obvious to me that not only myself but others that I went to church with and fellowshipped with were living lives of defeat, mediocrity, and a very unproductive spiritual walk with God that brought no excitement or personal fulfillment. Many people are in jeopardy of missing God's best due to a lack of understanding in regard to the power and wisdom available to us through Him in the Person of His Holy Spirit. It is amazing how one scripture in the Bible on an aisle of Family Dollar led me down a new road of discovery that forever changed my life. It is my hope that after reading this book, you too will find a new desire to seek the face of God and draw closer like never before to the Person of the Holy Spirit. The Holy Spirit desires to talk, lead, and guide you on an adventure like never before. You only have one chance here on earth to take a personal and intimate journey with the Holy Spirit. God Bless.

CHAPTER 1
What Do You Know About The Holy Spirit?

Years before the Lord began to deal with on inquiring more about the Person of the Holy Spirit, It was immediately obvious, that the ministry and importance of the Holy Spirit was neglected in so many ways because of ignorance and commitment to religious traditions. My personal thought process in my beginning walk with God placed the Spirit of God in a comfortable religious box. He was only expected, in my opinion, to appear on a regular basis in Sunday morning worship services or during my personal prayer times when I was alone with God. I had experienced many manifestations of His power in my personal life, but for the most part there was a general lack of personal awareness of how involved the Holy Spirit wanted to be in my everyday life.

He does not just want to meet you on certain designated Sunday's, in some chapel, during a set hour of corporate worship, but He wants to commune with you all day every day! The Holy Spirit wants to be involved in your family relationships, personal finances, cultivation of spiritual gifts, daily decisions, and even eating habits. I had the spiritual understanding and personal experience to know that the Holy Spirit dwelled on the inside of His believers, but I didn't know He was really that interested in every detail of our lives.

This new journey of faith in learning more about the ways of the Holy Spirit immediately challenged some of my personal understandings and beliefs as I am sure it will yours over the course of your reading this book. Now is the time to consider the possibility that your life can change forever as the lessons I have learned from the Holy Spirit over the years are imparted to you. From the ultimate role and purpose to the importance of the Holy Spirit and His significance in our personal lives and the world around us, He desires to lead, convict, and teach us in every area of our life if we are willing to allow Him to do so. There is not a problem too difficult that He cannot solve. Nor is there an answer that He does not know. He will lead you to make the right financial investments and even to select the correct college if you are willing to follow His lead.

This book was inspired by God to help motivate us in our seeking a deeper spiritual walk with His Spirit. First, before we begin to learn to understand the basic function of the Holy Spirit in our everyday life, it is imperative that we seek to understand the role of the Holy Spirit in our life from a new set of lenses. The Holy Spirit is not just some bystander sitting on the bench waiting to be called in from the sidelines and to help assist when things get difficult in life, although this is how some of us often treat Him.

The Holy Spirit one particular evening warned me about an associate from the neighborhood that I grew up with and with whom I had become reconnected in the course of time. My mother had travelled out of town to visit some relatives. She asked for me to stop by her apartment at least once a day to check in on it. On the second day of keeping watch, I was washing my hands in the restroom when the Holy Spirit spoke clearly to me saying, "Do not trust him!" The Holy Spirit actually spoke this guy's name to me. Before the Holy Spirit spoke these words to me, I admit that I had some personal suspicions regarding this guy's character. Over the few months that I was hanging around him, he started to ask for money and seemed to slip back into the lifestyle of chasing women, hanging around old associates from the neighborhood, and going to clubs. He seemed to quit every job he would start to work only about two months on the job. Less than a month later he went to prison for robbery. I never prayed when the Holy Spirit warned me about him. The voice of the Holy Spirit was so clear that afternoon that I did not second guess that I heard from Him. I made it a point to be on guard and watch his movements more closely from the moment I received the instructions. The last time I saw him what when I dropped him and a friend off at someone's house.

There was another particular time that the Holy Spirit spoke to me about another individual one morning and said, "Cancel the spirit of suicide." The voice of the Spirit was very clear that day as I arose out of bed. His voice seemed to ring in my spirit. The Holy Spirit repeated himself two to three times. I immediately began to pray. I then got dressed to head to work. I pondered the words of the Spirit but decided to pray for wisdom to confront the individual that He warned me about. Later during the day, an individual called me and confessed struggling with the thoughts of committing suicide. As I talked to the individual for a while. It was a lesson that I knew I would never forget. What if I did not heed the warning of the Holy Spirit that morning, what could have been the outcome? A premature death?

It is important for us to remember as we go

throughout our daily routine of the day that we must become and remain sensitive to His voice because not being obedient to the gentle prompting of the Holy Spirit could lead to someone's funeral or maybe our own. I will never forget this, and I pray that you understand that the Lord is willing to use you to help divert tragedy to those around you. Are you willing to listen closer to the words of the Holy Spirit? Jesus advised us in Revelation 2:7, "He who has an ear, let him hear what the Spirit says." What is the Spirit trying to communicate to you today?

There was also the time when the Holy Spirit gave me an impression in my mind early in the morning of three former students. The Spirit revealed to me that they were trying to devise a plan to get me in trouble on my job as an educator. I simply prayed about the Word spoken to me that morning and prepared myself for work. Later that day, the school counselor came to my room to share with me that three students were attempting to complain against me regarding my strict academic classroom environment. She informed me that she did not believe any of their allegations, but she wanted to make me aware of what was going on. This was the evidence I needed to prove that the Holy Spirit has a personal desire to give us guidance and instruction.

If we are willing to listen closely, He will help keep us from getting distracted and blinded by planned attacks from the enemy.

There have been times when the Holy Spirit warned me to be quiet in certain situations to avoid strife. It has also pleased the Holy Spirit at times to share unexpectedly the spiritual condition of a church. One afternoon, I was invited to support a fellow minister who I had once attended school with in elementary and middle school. I had preached at his church a few times before and was quite familiar with the congregation and pastor. While sitting in the pulpit, the voice of the Holy Spirit spoke these words to me suddenly, "There is a curse on this church." I knew I had heard the voice of the Spirit but did not say anything to anyone sitting in the pulpit. It made sense now from a natural perspective because over the sixteen years that I had been affiliated with this church, I noticed there was never a crowd of over thirty people during the Sunday morning worship service. Over time, the church declined in numbers and lacked the presence of God.

After service while in the pastor's study, I made the mistake of telling the minister I came to support and the pastor of the church what the Holy Spirit spoke to me in the pulpit. The pastor was irritated and visibly upset. Lesson learned! Sometimes when the Holy Spirit speaks to you, you are not to speak what He reveals to you. There will be times the Holy Spirit reveals things to you so that you can pray and intercede regarding the matter.

Though these are my some of my personal experiences with Him, there are many biblical accounts that support His desire to be an active participant in every area from the start of your day, character, business deals, as well as churches with whom we choose to worship with our families and our personal spiritual walk. While it may be helpful to hear how the Holy Spirit has worked in the lives of other believers throughout the world, this pales in comparison to the personal work of the Holy Spirit as He manifests in our daily life. Before my Dollar Tree encounter, He was not on my mind like that. As He began to draw me closer to see who He is and what He wanted to do in me and around me, my personal journey to seek in Him in prayer and through meticulous study began. As you read these pages, I have no doubt that the Holy Spirit will inspire you to want a more fulfilling and transformative relationship with Him.

When you make up in your mind to become truly intimate and consistent in your walk with the Holy Spirit, there will be nothing that you face or encounter that you will not be able to overcome if you use His divine wisdom. I have come to know that The Holy Spirit is the most overlooked part of God and as a result of not engaging Him, many people fail to maximize their full potential before they leave this earth. This can be avoided by truly understanding and utilizing the divine advantage that you uniquely have at your fingertips with the supernatural knowledge and intervention of God's Spirit. The Spirit has a Personality, multiple attributes, and diversity of roles that He fulfills in the life of a Christian at any given time. Counselor. Teacher. Guide.

CHAPTER 2
The Holy Spirit Has A History

The first mention of the Holy Spirit can be found in Genesis 1:2 which says, "the Spirit of God moved upon the face of the waters." This scripture introduces us to the unmatched divine creativity of the Holy Spirit, as He was personally involved in the creation of the earth. The Bible states in Genesis 1:26-27, that the Holy Spirit was also involved in the sculpting of Adam, "Then God said, "Let Us make man in Our image..." It was interesting for me to take note that the Holy Spirit is such a creative force that He has the ability to create something from nothing.

I was always under the assumption during my early years of walking with God, that the Holy Spirit mainly operated in the New Testament. I would eventually read excerpts in the Old Testament that would challenge my earlier beliefs. In Ezekiel 36:27, it reads, "I will put my Spirit within you and cause you to walk in My statutes, and you will keep My judgements and do them." However, in the Old Testament the Holy Spirit also operated in the life of the priests, kings, judges, and even prophets at random times to assist supernaturally in helping them fulfill their appointed tasks.

Let us explore the example of Samson. According to Judges 15:6, "The Spirit of the Lord came powerfully upon him so that he tore the lion apart with his bare hands as he might have torn a young goat." Before Samuel was anointed the first king of Israel, 1 Samuel 10:10 records that, "the Spirit of God came upon him, and he prophesied among them." During the dispensations throughout the Old Testament, the Holy Spirit worked in the life of the followers of God by inspiring them to prophesy, leading them with divine direction, filling the temple during times of worship, etc.

During the New Testament, the Holy Spirit appears after the promise of Christ to His devoted followers. In John 14:1-17, Jesus teaches His disciples about the future, "And I will pray Father, and He will give another Helper, that He may abide with you forever, - the Spirit of truth, whom the world cannot receive, because it neither knows Him; but you know Him, for

He dwells with you and will be in you." This gives us a promise from Christ that His Spirit would not only abide within us, but the Holy Spirit would be a Helper and a Spirit that manifests truth in our life. In the Book of Acts, the Holy Spirit not only baptizes believers in the Upper Room, He also directs the apostles on their missionary journeys, provides spiritual discernment, selects the disciple's spiritual gifts, and even assists them in their ministry with the demonstration of supernatural miracles.

It is important for me to let you know that an individual cannot learn everything about the power, function, role, attributes, and ways of the Holy Spirit overnight. It is a methodical process that you must experience by intentionally engaging in the spiritual disciplines of reading your Bible, meditating in the scriptures, prayer, fasting, corporate worship, and personal study. These must be coupled with having a willing heart to know the Holy Spirit in a greater measure than before.

Have you ever thought about the fact that the Holy Spirit is willing to strategically assist you with any problem you are currently facing? The challenges of unexpected obstacles, financial debt, hostile work environments, personal misdirection, marital problems, ministry detours, or even issues that you may be facing with your children can all be resolved by asking the

Holy Spirit to reveal a solution to your problem. Unfortunately, this revelation concerning the ability and willingness of the Spirit to work alongside us and help transform our life is something that took nearly a decade for me to realize. However, if you will but cultivate a relationship with Him, you will not only learn more about the Holy Spirit but take part in a journey here on earth that you will never regret.

CHAPTER 3
The Holy Spirit Helps With Conversion

It was in 2001, the late fall of my first semester as a sophomore at Morehouse College, when I accepted Jesus Christ as my personal Savior. It was a normal humid Georgia afternoon day. After my last academic class of the day, it was a routine for some of the fellows to get together off campus and smoke weed. My former dorm room mate and myself, met in front of the campus post office which was our daily routine throughout the week. We were the only ones free after class, so we decided to take the usual stroll off campus into the surrounding neighborhood to smoke marijuana. On this particular day, we made small talk about current events that were taking place in America, campus news, ladies, and personal issues we were facing at the time which was nothing unusual. The sky was blue, and the wind gave us brief relief in spite of the humid temperatures.

Halfway through our conversation, he mentioned taking a required religion course to fulfill his credits in humanities for his college degree. He informed me that his imagination was captured in class while the professor was explaining the Old Testament story of the patriarch Job. I listened attentively as the smoke came out of my nose. My friend from the Mid-West explained with the enthusiasm of someone that stumbled upon a new-found life changing discovery about this man who had lost everything. This biblical figure lost his children, flock of animals, marriage, real estate, esteemed name, and health. Sitting back smoking and listening to my old friend talk about this ancient figure from biblical history was holding my attention. I couldn't help but become enamored with his discovery of this story in the Bible. Before we departed ways, he also told me how this man named Job endured great satanic persecution and affliction. As we shook hands and departed ways, my mind seemed to be set on looking more into this story.

While walking back to campus, I couldn't help but think of this story I just heard. My friend was not the religious type in any way at all, which is why this stuck with me the entire walk back to the dorm room. The inspiration to read my Bible that my grandmother purchased for me before I started college was something new to me. I hadn't opened my Bible in at least four months. The particles of brown dust and dirt scattered everywhere as I finally lifted the Bible from its secure location on my desk in the dorm room.

The only thing I knew at the time was that the story of this man named Job could be located somewhere in the pages of the Old Testament. As I begin to search for this centuries' old story of tragedy and triumph, piercing silence seemed to invade my second floor dorm room without an invitation. It was destined for it to be just me and the dusty covered Bible without any interruption from my roommate. I finally found the story in the Bible after two minutes of diligently searching through the unruffled pages. Immediately, after reading the story of Job, I found myself on my knees pleading for God's mercy in my life. The more that I read about the life of Job and his personal trials of faith, I could not help but see the obvious parallel between Job's boils and the boils that had just recently left my torso after seven weeks of incurable pain during my summer break in 2001.

My constant companions at the time were marijuana and a mind bombarded with continued regrets from the decisions of my youth. However, after reading this story in the Bible, I found myself crying out for a life of peace and grace that could only be granted from a sovereign God. I so desperately wanted to get back to the days of my youth when I use to continuously beg my mother to take me to midweek youth bible study. As I mustered the personal strength and energy to ask God to forgive me of my sins and enter into my life, I will never forget that specific moment in time. It changed the course of my life forever! Sobbing uncontrollably, I felt the presence of something unseen hovering over me and filling me up on the inside. Dear reader, this was the beginning of my personal introduction to my relationship with the Holy Spirit. Right away I sensed that something was different on the inside of my soul. There was a cleansing process that took place to the very depths of my inward parts as the Holy Spirit entered into my life on that day, right in my dorm room, the fall of 2001 in Atlanta.

The first few days after my dramatic spiritual conversion with the infilling of the Holy Spirit was pleasant. I walked around the campus with a new found sense of peace and love within my heart. Others that knew me best immediately recognized the difference. However, it wasn't until I was reading my Bible in my dorm room later that I stumbled upon the discovery of what had really occurred just a few days prior when I became born again. While sitting at the desk in my dorm, I read the words of Luke the physician in Acts 2:4, "All of them were filled with the Holy Spirit..." I felt like a new man and there was a change within that could not be readily explained theologically at the time but with the assistance of the Holy Spirit, I was a new creation in Christ Jesus.

Those around me, even my closest friends immediately recognized the drastic change in my life. How could they not see? I had abruptly stopped smoking, drinking, partying, hanging out, and even hanging with the guys. If I was not in class, I was either eating, studying, reading the Bible, fellowshipping with Christians on campus in the Christian Youth Fellowship, or attending church (whenever I could take a break from schoolwork). My main objective was trying to find more understanding and clarity about this new found spiritual experience that unexpectedly revolutionized my life starting with the ministry of the Holy Spirit.

It is the Holy Spirit that convicts the inhabitants in this world of sin. Jesus stated in John 16:8, "When He (Holy Spirit) comes, He will convict the world of its sin, and God's righteousness, and of the coming judgement". When we experience the conviction of the Holy Spirit, we only have two choices here on earth, we can either resist the conviction of Him or decide to submit our will to Him. The Holy Spirit is a willing participant in every conversion that has taken place with His followers.

CHAPTER 4
Lessons Learned Along The Way

My new found conversion motivated me to read any spiritual book I could put my hand on and query every mature Christian that would listen to me about how to walk closer to God. This lasted for nearly a year, before I returned to some of my former ways. When I repented of my sins the fall of 2001 in my dorm room, I was immediately baptized with the Holy Spirit. I did not know what you called it at the time. This is the thing that has often bothered me as I have matured in my journey with Christ. As much as I attended church in my youth and teenage days, why didn't anyone I know inform me of the power and divine enabling ability of the Spirit to strengthen me against sin? One of the things that we must be cognizant of is that sin has the ability to pull us back into the destructive habits of our past. That is why it is imperative that we learn how to follow the Holy Spirit's leadings and promptings. This ability often comes with time and quality fellowship with Him.

I heard the Holy Spirit mentioned in a few sermons while growing up, but I did not really know who He was or what His importance was in the life of a believer. I believe that many of those in the church today could have prevented some delays, business failures, divorces, and misdirection in life if they knew the Holy Spirit was willing to help them. That is why it is so critical that you understand that the greatest asset that you have available concerning your present life issues is the teaching that can only come from the Holy Spirit.

There was no church member that pulled me aside to explain and even disciple me step by step, concerning how to follow or listen to the voice of the Holy Spirit. In the days of my early ministry, there was a time of frustration when I would explain to my grandmother about my desire for a spiritual mentor even though there have been seasons when the Lord would place strong men of God in my life. My grandmother would always say to me, "Could it possibly be that the Lord wants to raise you up Himself?"

It took some time to really develop and tune my ear

to understand how and when the Spirit of God was speaking to me. Reading the Bible is very important in your development in hearing the voice of the Spirit. This will allow your inner spirit to be fed by God's Word and give free reign to the Spirit of God to minister to you the things He desires to communicate. As you spend time in reading the Word of God, you must also engage in consecrated personal prayer. The Holy Spirit speaks to me more profoundly during my personal time in prayer. There are times when I immediately know what He is saying to me and other times I have to wait for clarity concerning what He has spoken. The more you spend time in prayer and devotion you will find yourself becoming more familiar with the voice of the Holy Spirit. Sometimes the Holy Spirit will have spoken and what He said came to pass an hour later or maybe a few weeks later. That's why it's important for you to seek the face of God in prayer and develop a personal devotional time with the Lord so that the Holy Spirit can speak to you concerning things that He wants you to know.

One of the most important lessons for you to understand early on while reading this book is that the Holy Spirit wants you to learn about Him from Him! Even though I have spent many years studying the Holy Spirit, I still listen to teachings about Him, read books, and articles about Him. The greatest teacher about the Holy Spirit is the Holy Spirit Himself. So, I make it a daily practice every morning when I wake up to ask Him to speak to me concerning anything He desires to share with me because I earnestly desire and need to know. He communicates to me in different ways and during various times of the day. I have heard the voice of the Holy Spirit in the shower, driving the car on the highway, while worshipping in the church, while asleep during a dream, through the voice of someone else, while praying for others, in the midst of preaching, and even during the early morning hours right before I wake up while still lying on my bed.

In the early stages of my walk with God, while an undergraduate student in Atlanta, there were a few things that caught my attention. Many Christians were so distracted and wrapped in their own selves and personal agenda that if you asked them when was the last time that the Lord had spoken to them, they wouldn't even be able to give you a decent reply. More than a few would tell me that they don't even know when God speaks to them. This should be a major issue of concern for the Body of Christ. It has concerned me over the years that I have encountered many Christians young and old that do not know the Holy Spirit on a personal basis much less are they aware that He even speaks to them. One of the things that the Lord placed on my heart over a decade ago was to prepare myself because there would be a time when I would mentor both young and seasoned

Christians. This book is aimed for those in Christ who seek a deeper understanding and revelation of the Holy Spirit. Each day that you wake up you should have a certain sense of expectation to have the Holy Spirit use you to speak prophetically into someone's life or to help someone solve a major dilemma that they are facing. One of the greatest ways to make sure you are walking into your destiny is to develop the ability to be led and directed by the Holy Spirit. It takes time, sacrifice, and humility to learn the lessons from Him along the way!

CHAPTER 5
Correct Understanding Of The Holy Spirit

Years ago, after praying at the church one afternoon concerning personal matters, I received the confirmation that "it seemed good to the Holy Spirit" (Acts 15:28), for me to write this book in to encourage His people to develop a stronger faith and walk with Him. Also, this book was created with the hopes to challenge and correct some of the false doctrinal teaching that has invaded the Body of Christ in regard to the Holy Spirit. Some Christians today, are under the false theological belief that the Holy Spirit can be easily taken from us, especially if we sin and do things that are unholy. Dead wrong! We live in the dispensation of grace and are not able to lose the Holy Spirit. We may sin and grieve the Holy Spirit; however, the Holy Spirit can never be taken from us. He is there to dwell on the inside of us as a Counselor and Guide.

Many who believe this unscriptural teaching came up under ministries that taught the false doctrine that refer to the words of King David in the Old Testament when pleading with God to not take His Holy Spirit from him. Some ministers and Christians automatically refer to the words of King David after he committed adultery with Bathsheba and the premeditated murder of her husband Uriah on the battlefield. David records his poetic lament in Psalm 51:11 with the words, "Do not cast me from your presence, or take your Holy Spirit from me". David was referring to the tangible presence and fellowship he had with the Holy Spirit that could be taken away when he sinned before God, not the permanent removal of the relationship and continual presence of the Holy Spirit of God that is ever with us.

During this time period in ancient Israel, the Holy Spirit worked within and alongside His chosen people to accomplish specific divine tasks. There would be times when the Holy Spirit would come upon God's prophets to prophesy to His people on certain occasions. God would use His prophets to give warning and results of war at times. The Prophet Micaiah in the 22nd chapter of 1st Kings, was responsible for prophesying defeat at the hands of the enemy. There were times when people in high political position often sought the advice of the prophet in regard to military strategy for upcoming wars. The Spirit of God was also used in the life of God's chosen people to accomplish specific tasks. There was a man by the name of Bezalel that was endowed with the "Spirit of God, with wisdom, understanding, with knowledge and with various kinds of skills, to design artistic works in gold, silver, and bronze." Exodus 31:3 - 5

On the Day of Pentecost, the disciple's lives were personally transformed when the house they were congregating in at the time was invaded by heaven through the power of prayer. The Bible informs us that "they were all filled with the Holy Spirit", (Acts 2:4). It is so important for us to understand this moment in the timeline of the history of the church. We have been graced with the distinct privilege of having close intimacy with the Holy Spirit and that should not be taken for granted. Jesus was recorded as saying in John 14:16, "And I will pray the Father, and he shall give you another Comforter, that He may abide with you forever". The word abide, in the Greek, means to stay and remain.

So what Jesus was doing here was endowing His followers with prophetic insight into the future role the Holy Spirit would play in their lives. The role and function of the Holy Spirit is to not just be with us, but to dwell within us. Do you see the powerful revelation in these words of scripture? This is an eternal promise given to every born-again believer in Jesus Christ. We no longer have to ever worry about God being far away from us during times of distress, family discord, physical problems, danger, or personal failure. For He will remain in us and dwell on the inside of all of His children. He is our God and we must be faithful to walk with the Divine counsel and wisdom of the Holy Spirit.

CHAPTER 6
The Holy Spirit Is Willing To Teach You

There is something extremely significant in spiritual substance regarding the words Jesus spoke while conducting an impromptu tutorial lesson with His disciples, "the Helper, the Holy Spirit, whom the Father will send in my name, He will teach you all things, and bring to your remembrance all things that I said to you." Here is Jesus, God in the flesh, informing His followers that the Holy Spirit will have the unique ability to teach us everything that we will need to know in our lifetime. ...Everything we need to know? Everything! The Holy Spirit is willing to lead us to pick the correct stock to invest in, which car to purchase at the dealership, and even which relationships to avoid in the workplace. I remember a few years ago I was driving to Arlington, Texas to meet up with a salesman at a local car dealership. As I was exiting the freeway, the Holy Spirit said to me, "Don't purchase that car!" I was less than a minute away from the car dealership, so I decided to go ahead and check out the car anyway. After walking through the car parking lot, I decided to pick a Chrysler to test drive. Not even five minutes into the car ride, I noticed the car did not ride smoothly on the roads. I made a comment to the salesman, but I already had my mind made up. I was going to drive back to the dealership and simply let the salesman know I was not interested.

I was already warned by the Holy Spirit not to buy the car. There will be certain times when the Holy Spirit will give you a clear order not to do something and you must obey His voice. Who knows what could have happened after I purchased that Chrysler? It could have broken down a few months after my purchase with extreme mechanical issues. It could have been an increased car payment, or maybe it would have had to be taken back to the dealership due to recalled parts. This would have been even a major problem due to my needing a car to get to work, transport my family around the city, and attend ministry events. Whatever the reason the Holy Spirit prevented me from purchasing the car on that particular day, I was obedient to His voice and avoided any unnecessary problems that could have derived from the purchase of that automobile. Obedience to the Holy Spirit helped me avoid any unnecessary trouble that He foresaw ahead of time.

Recently, there was an article in a popular religious magazine quoting a professor from a religious institution in the United States that stated Christians should not seek guidance from the Holy Spirit in making major decisions in life such as choosing jobs, making important financial decisions, or even relying on Him to discern the mate that God has chosen for you to marry. This is foolish. It is not a matter of why we should but why shouldn't we let the Holy Spirit direct every affair of our life. As humans, we are limited in our understanding of everything around us. How many times have you made life altering mistakes that could have been simply avoided if you allowed yourselves to be led by the Holy Spirit? Proverbs 16:9 declares, "A man's heart plans his way, But the Lord directs his steps." I wonder did this professor ever make some mistakes that altered the course of his life. So many things could be avoided in our life if we discipline ourselves to learning what the Spirit is leading us to do in certain situations. If the Son of God Himself, said that one of the main purposes of the Spirit is to teach and instruct us, it makes perfect sense to follow the words of Jesus and become a student of the Holy Spirit.

Let me share a few examples of how the Spirit has led me to make the correct decisions unexpectedly.

One day the principal at a school I once worked at walked into the room to conduct a teacher evaluation. As I was silently praying for guidance and favor with the lessons that I was about to begin teaching to the students in the classroom, seemingly out of nowhere, the Spirit of God spoke to me directly and suggested to me the lesson I should teach that day to the class. I had three lessons prepared at the time. I was obedient to the leading of the Holy Spirit and taught the class the presentation selected by Him. The lesson flowed smoothly without any problems and I received a high rating on my evaluation. When the principal left the classroom forty minutes after the start of my presentation, I silently thanked the Lord for His guidance on that day.

Another time, I was trying to discern the will of God about a particular young lady that I was dating at the time. I just couldn't figure out if this young lady was the woman I needed to settle down with for the rest of my life. So, after praying consistently for some weeks and seeking wise spiritual counsel, one day while at a theme park, in the midst of the rides, food, and games, I heard the silent still voice of the Holy Spirit teach me something. He told me, "She is just a friend." I immediately recognized the voice of the Spirit speaking to me. At the time, I was saddened but years later I was thankful that I obeyed the voice of the Spirit. You see, often times the Holy Spirit is more than willing to speak to us about everything that we need to know and even things we haven't thought of or encountered at the time. He is always willing to lend His expertise in any matter that we are facing and need help. You must learn how to position yourself, not only just in prayer and fasting, but with a desire from your heart to want to receive direction from the Holy Spirit. Nehemiah recorded these words, "You also gave your good Spirit to instruct them." (Nehemiah 9:20). Let us learn how to receive specific instruction from the Spirit regarding the everyday affairs our life, small and big.

CHAPTER 7
The Spirit Will Provide Direction

It takes only one direction given to you from the Holy Spirit to change present day circumstances or even the trajectory of your life. There are Christians today who feel overwhelmed, depressed, and frustrated concerning their present circumstance just like I once was about my past. I was once so low that I lost the will to even wake up in the morning and face life head on. I did not have a job, bank account, a car and I was staying at my Grandmother's house. I had completely stopped going to church and found myself spiraling downward into a pit of alcoholism. God eventually pulled me through that season of heartache and darkness, as I obeyed His leading to return to reading the word of God and seeking wise counsel. One of the lessons you must glean concerning following the leading of the Spirit for direction, is that you must be patient and sensitive to the voice of the Spirit. He will speak but you must be attentive to the small still voice of the Holy Spirit when He does speak. You can cultivate an ear to hear the Holy Spirit by establishing a lifestyle of consistent prayer, Bible reading, fasting, listening to sermons, and worship. There would be times when the Holy Spirit would speak, and I would receive divine revelations and visitations from God even when I would go months without prayer and Bible devotion. This was a unique season of my life that I personally believe the Lord allowed through which he extended grace to get me through the that extremely dry time.

So often times, people within the Body of Christ, fail to rely on the divine benefit of being filled with the Spirit. It is my belief that many Christians have not been properly trained and taught on the divine advantage the Holy Spirit gives us in our personal life. We have, due to church tradition, restricted the Holy Spirit to corporate worship on Sunday and His manifestation during the preaching of the Word of God. These two examples are very vital for the health and progress of the local church. However, the Holy Spirit has a much more extensive role in the life of a Christian that just that. The Spirit of the Lord has an willing desire to direct our life's paths, reveal mysteries, assist in solving problems, and personally give solutions for perplexing issues that we cannot solve on our own.

The Holy Spirit when He speaks, only communicates truth to us. Jesus refers to the Holy Spirit, in John 16:13, as the "Spirit of Truth". I believe that one of the reasons that many of us fail to take our leading from the Holy Spirit is either because we unaware that He is willing to lead us even in the small matters of life or because what He speaks to us is contrary to what we desire to hear from Him regarding a particular situation. Whenever the Holy Spirit communicates to us regarding anything, it will always be the truth! We can either submit to what the Spirit of Truth is telling us to do or choose to accomplish our own desire. We as Christians more than not choose the latter option when we are making critical decisions in life.

It is imperative that you take the necessary time to position yourself to hear and heed the direction of the Spirit in every area of your life. Remember the time I shared with you when I was unemployed, in financial crisis, I had no debit card, no bank account, had to borrow my mother's car for transportation, and I was even labeled a deadbeat dad because I had absolutely nothing but the clothes on my back for my earthly possessions, along with a substantial amount of books I had acquired over the years since college. I knew that I had to make a drastic change… and quickly. I felt ashamed that I had to ask my mother for money to get a haircut, or for gas money just to put into the car that she was graciously letting me drive until I got on my feet. That was a terrible place to be. The only thing I could do was pray and believe that God would give specific direction to help me get back on my feet. It was through this time of intense prayer that the Holy Spirit began to speak to me about the direction I needed to go that would lead me into the educational path and ultimately the career He had designed me for.

You have to understand how God operates. God has a uniqueness in answering prayers in the least likely of ways. I asked God for a job and He blessed me to make minimum wage in a warehouse. It is important to note that I had to put in the footwork to find the job. Every day or so I would drive around town and place applications at jobs and even temporary agencies. After a few months working as a porter in an apartment complex making just nine dollars a hour, I was disgruntled with this job so I started working in a warehouse for a few months. Tired of getting up at three in the morning to make it to work on time, I knew God had something better in store for me, but I just didn't know what it was at the time. I went back to the Lord in prayer and asked Him for specific direction a few months later but this time I simply told God that I wanted a career. It was very frustrating at times working in a hot and humid warehouse with a college degree standing on my feet all the time with mandatory overtime on Saturdays. This was not the route I wanted to go with my life. At the time, I had three children and I needed to provide some sort of financial income for their needs, but I didn't have enough finances to support myself. While working in the factory, I had the tedious task of testing cellular phones to make sure their batteries were working. This was surely not the reason I accumulated debt while in college.

One day, I ran into a lady putting up a sign on a marquee outside of a small house less than a mile away from my grandmother's house. After pulling over to talk to her for a few minutes, she invited me to bible study the following weekend at that same house. After the bible study that following Saturday, I was talking to the lady that invited me to the bible study but overheard a man tell another individual that he was a retired teacher. When he said the word teacher, it was as if the Holy Spirit arrested my attention. Immediately, I knew that the Lord was speaking to me to enter into the field of education. Something in my spirit knew that the Lord had provided an answer to my previous prayers of wanting a fulfilling career to help provide financial stability for my family.

Eight years later as an educator in the public-school system, I began to sense a transition taking place in my life. After years of walking and learning from the Holy

Spirit, the first thing I have learned is that sometimes there will be restlessness when God is trying to get your attention regarding moves, He desires for you to make in your personal journey with Him. When you begin to sense a time of restlessness, this is the time to pray and seek guidance from the Holy Spirit concerning the next steps you need to take in your life. You will discern moments in your walk with the Lord when you can't even actually explain how the Lord is giving you specific direction, but within your heart you know that He is guiding you to make a decision and it doesn't make sense. Whether its changing jobs, choosing a house to live in, business ideas, and ministry assignments, we must seek the Holy Spirit to direct us in the clear and precise steps to take. To this day, there are times when I am disappointed for not following the leading of the Holy Spirit in my personal life.

There was a time during my senior year of college that I felt led to put in a application to Princeton Theological Seminary. I hesitated for a few weeks but eventually decided to not put in the application. What resulted was a year of regret and questioning myself if life would have turned out differently if I decided to pursue a theological education at Princeton. One lesson I have learned over the years, is to follow my natural instinct when I sense the Lord is directing me to take a particular path in life even if I'm not absolutely sure of direction I need to take at that moment. I have grieved at times regarding the failure to follow the leading of the Holy Spirit, but this has brought about within me, a firmer determination to follow the Spirit not knowing what the final outcome will be in the end.

There are times when you can receive direction from the Holy Spirit while reading the Bible. Often times, a scripture will seem to jump off the page at you while reading. It is never coincidence when a scripture speaks to the very thing that you are experiencing at that precise moment in time that your needing assistance with it. There have been times when I have read the Bible and a certain passage of scripture stood out to me by the Holy Spirit. It was only later on during the day when I would run into a certain situation that I would begin to understand why the Holy Spirit highlighted a particular scripture while I was reading the Bible. When it comes to receiving direction from the Spirit of God, there are no certain guidelines to follow. You must be willing to keep an open heart and discerning spirit to be led by Him. The Holy Spirit can give you direction while watching television, listening to a sermon on a podcast, inner conviction, or a dream. There is something that must be taken into serious consideration when following the leading of the Spirit of God. You must be willing to obey in faith, trusting that the Lord knows what He is doing at all times. There will be times when the Holy Spirit speaks to you and it does not make sense. Just trust and obey God knowing that He sees what you cannot perceive and understands all things. God desires to bless you and direct you toward your destiny and personal calling in Him.

CHAPTER 8
The Holy Spirit Reveals His Will For Your Life

The Holy Spirit has been relegated to just a spiritual presence or manifestation on Sundays during church. He is so much more than that in our life. He is truly a Helper, Guide, and Counselor if we allow Him to just direct us in our personal life. The Holy Spirit has every answer to every problem you will every face in life. He is willing to guide you and your family to your next destination if you are willing to seek His perfect will. We often waste years in the desert like the Israelites of Moses day, going around the mountain of doubt, indecisiveness, wrong turns, and setbacks. The only answer for a lack of progress in every area of our life is choosing to submit to the will of God that the Holy Spirit is just waiting to reveal to each one of us if we take the time to seek Him.

Have you ever thought how life would be, if you were free from debt, able to select the correct job, marry the right person, go to the college God selects for you, and allow God to help you create a business? Sometimes I believe we are so caught up in our life and the world around us, that we fail to acknowledge that God is not far removed from our everyday activities. In fact, He is carefully observing every move that we make. The Bible instructs us in Proverbs 5:21, "For your ways are in full view of the Lord, and he examines all your ways."

Over the years as I sought the Lord more in prayer and fasting. He would reveal Himself in some of the strangest ways to reveal His divine will regarding certain situations. One humid Texas afternoon while sitting in my grandmother's room in the back of her house, my grandmother told me of the time when she was shopping at the neighborhood grocery store for a few groceries. She told me that she decided to pick up a few items for the house, while shopping she turned down the aisle after selecting a few items to pick up a package of meat. She felt the Holy Spirit prompt her not to buy the meat. She totally disregarded the prompting of the Holy Spirit, that was attempting to stir her away from buying that particular package of meat. She cooked the meat later that night only to find her stomach upset with constant pains. She felt led by the Lord to go check the expiration date on the package. The meat was expired, and the consequence was food poisoning that lasted for days. The meat had been expired three days prior to her buying it at the grocery store. As she recanted this story to me in her room, I marveled at the fact that the Spirit is willing to even led us in the proper selection of food if we allow Him to guide us even at the grocery store.

I remember vividly another time that the Spirit of God led me to make a particular decision in regard to a person I was introduced to some years ago. One day while driving down the street, I pulled over to give a donation to a church selling baked goods. Before I departed, the lady informed me that there was a young lady that she wanted me to meet. I passed my number along and decided to wait on the young lady to call me that afternoon. I thought to myself, what would it hurt to get introduced to a young lady that was a Christian and had a desire to serve the Lord such as myself. The young lady called that night and we had a good conversation for hours on the telephone. Before we hung up the phone, she informed me that during our conversation that a voice told her during the beginning of our conversation that I was her husband. Interesting I thought to myself. We decided to talk the following day and select a location to meet up when time permitted during the next few days. A few days later we set up a time and location to meet up at on the weekend. The day that I was to meet her, I was shaving in the bathroom when the Holy Spirit said to me, "Don't go!" I knew immediately that I heard the voice of the Spirit. I hesitated for a moment but decided to go see her anyway. I met up with the young lady and sat down to talk with her for over a hour while eating hamburgers at Whataburger. By the end of the conversation, it was obvious why the Holy Spirit directed me not to meet this young lady. She was being deceived by her spiritual leader and living a life of delusion. Something in my spirit knew that something was not correct with the story of her life events. There was an uneasiness in my spirit during our conversation. After I politely walked her to her car, I decided to myself it would be best to block all communication with this young lady. I got in my car and while driving down the street, I received a call from this young lady. The very sentence that came out of her mouth slightly shocked me. She indicated to me that before she left her residence, something told her not to come. I immediately agreed with her and wished her the best in life. A few days later her spiritual leader that presented herself as a pastor called me one night asking for money for her ministry. I knew that was not of God. This so-called pastor was a manipulator and deceiver. I got off the phone and blocked her number.

We must not only be willing to be led by the Spirit but trust Him in the process of following Him. God can help avoid delays and detours in life that we hinder us from reaching our destiny. We have to understand that God is omniscient, He knows everything. He knows the intents of people hearts, final outcomes, and strategies we should implement to reach our goals. You must cultivate a heart that is willing to obey the Spirit when He is speaking and be willing to allow the Holy Spirit to guide you in every situation. The Holy Spirit protected me from this young lady. The Holy Spirit is able to clearly discern the hidden agendas and personal motives of people before we even have the chance to figure out when something is not right. The following night after our brief meeting at the fast food restaurant, the young lady called me to inform me that I was being disobedient to God. My disobedience was a result of me choosing to not to pay her pastor's car note. I was astonished to say the least at what just came out of her mouth. Here I was making sure my car payment was being turned in on time (barely) and now all of a sudden I didn't know that God was requiring me to pay her pastors car note at the same time. Foolish as it may seem, I was not willing to fall into this trap.

How many times have we heard stories of people being manipulated and extorted of money from so called religious leaders that lived off the hard work of its followers? I was laughing out loud while on the phone when she informed me of my transgressions before God for the failure to pay her pastor's car note.

My heart immediately went out to this young lady who was caught in the bondage of religious manipulation from this so-called church leader. I could not help but to think about the multitudes of people following seducing spirits and false teachers across the world. I failed to follow the leading of the Spirit at first by meeting with the young lady, but eventually it was so evident that I needed to steer as far away from this young lady and her pastor as possible. It is very important to not only discern the voice of the Spirit but to obey His commands as well because He will prompt us the right way to choose every time.

CHAPTER 9
A Lesson In Being Led By The Spirit

When I accepted Jesus Christ into my life as a sophomore in college. I never knew that the Christian journey ahead of me would consist of so many unexpected twists, hardships, tests, and turns along the way. For so many of you walking with the Lord, it is critical that you always acknowledge that the enemy of your destiny is Satan. He has shrewdly constructed and devised weapons to destroy not only your destiny, but your mind, happiness, family, finances, health, and personal integrity. One day while reading my Bible during devotion, I was led by the Holy Spirit to read Romans 8:14, "for those who are led by the Spirit of God, are the children God." The was the very first time that I read this scripture with a sense of purpose. I found myself pondering as a new Christian at the time, how does the Lord really lead His people? I understood that there had to be a purpose for why God placed these words within the pages of the Bible.

One day I was standing outside all by myself, trying to figure out how in the world anyone could be led by the Spirit. As soon as I was thinking this in my mind, there was a gentle breeze of wind that came out of nowhere. Immediately, I understood the words in Romans 8:14. Following the Holy Spirit, is just like following the wind that blows on the earth. You never know when or where the wind will blow, but you must be willing to follow its direction when it does blow in a specific direction. The most important step in learning to be led by the Spirit of God is having a heart and true desire deep from within to follow Him wherever He leads. Whether you are actively engaged in full time ministry, a computer programmer, involved in politics, a manager at a retail outlet, or a stay at home mom devoted to raising your kids, the Holy Spirit is willing to lead you in every area of your life.

There was a time when I stayed in Ogden, Utah with an older cousin by the name of Dennis Carpenter. It was a time of rest and inner healing for me. One Sunday morning, I decided to visit a church and by divine providence I just so happened to be sitting in the back of the church when my attention was drawn to two things. First, I noticed an old high school classmate of mine that was playing basketball at Weber

State University. We had not spoken in years and were more than surprised to run into each other. The second thing that stood out to me that evening in the back of the church was a pencil that I found in the middle of the seat cushion with the word Texas printed on its side. A few weeks prior to visiting this church, I sensed that it was time for me to move back home and start my life over. Crossing paths with my former classmate and finding a pencil printed with the word Texas to me were signs that I needed to head back home. We must be aware of the different methods and ways God will use to get our attention to led us. The Contemporary Version of the Bible states in Job 33:4, "God speaks in different ways, and we don't always recognize His voice." God is diverse in His ability to communicate. I have always been intrigued by how God speaks to people in a variety of ways. A lady that I had been knowing since I was a young boy told me one afternoon that God always spoke to her through the movies she watched. Another pastor, I've observed over the years, always sensed an inner impression from within the inside, when He sensed God leading him to pray for someone who was sick.

My experience with the Holy Spirit has provided me with a few spiritual insights to share with you. You must understand that the leading of the Holy Spirit is unpredictable at times. You will never know how and when He will choose to direct you down a particular path, career, transition, or ministry call. He uses dreams, visions, scriptures, counsel of wise Christian's, parents, circumstances, and everyday normal conversation to lead you in life. Your number one priority is to follow Him by faith. Following God will not even make sense at times. I've often noticed in my personal life, that the Spirit of God will lead me down paths that I least expected. It may sometimes be the road that you least likely expected. You must be willing to risk everything to follow the Holy Spirit's leading to reach His intended destination for your life.

I can vividly remember when after my first year after college, I was staying in Austell, Georgia, right outside of Atlanta. I was coming to the end of my substitute assignment with the Cobb County School district and I did not know what to do. I did not have any job prospects lined up. Most likely, because not only I wasn't putting in any job applications at all. I was struggling with just being motivated. I had looked for a few jobs in the area, but I just knew deep inside of me that my time was coming to a close in Atlanta.

One day I called my boyhood pastor, Dr. B.R Daniels Jr. I'll never forget how after I explained my financial struggles and lack of job opportunities. He simply said, "Well, Patrick, read the story of the Prophet Elijah. There are times that God will dry things up in your life when He is trying to move you from one location to another." He began to review with careful detail and the wisdom of an old seasoned pastor how the Old Testament story of the prophet Elijah could be beneficial for me to study and meditate on during that season of my life. Strategic lessons on how God divinely guided the Prophet Elijah to the brook and supernaturally provided the ravens to bring him food to eat. God intentionally guided Elijah to another location, the widow's home by drying up his resources of provision from the brook. As my boyhood pastor was telling me the story. In my spirit, I sensed the Lord telling me that it was time to pack up my bags and prepare to leave Atlanta and relocate to my hometown of Fort Worth, Texas. I didn't hesitate nor did I struggle internally with any mix feelings regarding the move that the Lord placed in my spirit to make. I had a sense of peace knowing that the Holy Spirit had spoken though my former pastor and that His words were my divine instruction from the Lord.

After I returned back to Texas, many of my neighborhood friends and even family members questioned my return back to the city of my birth. The only thing I could say to myself during the rough days of having no job, car, ministry engagements, and future career prospects was that I was in the perfect will of God for my life. I wasn't in Fort Worth two months, when I was offered a job while riding in the back of my church van headed out of town to celebrate a pastor's anniversary in East Texas. You must understand that if God dries up one place in your life, the Holy Spirit will redirect you to the next place of provision, location, career, or ministry assignment. You must be willing to be led by the Holy Spirit in every area of your life. God has the ability to see what we can't see. For us to live a victorious life on a consistent basis, we must learn how to be led by the Holy Spirit every day.

It takes time and deliberate effort to follow after God at all cost. This is something totally contrary to the world's way of thinking. We have been raised and nurtured in a world in which we are conditioned to try our way first and then when that doesn't seem to work out, we often find ourselves at the mercy seat of God begging for advice and divine assistance. Usually in a posture of defeat and weariness, with arms extended to heaven asking for Him to deliver us out of the mess we created that could have been avoided if we would have sought the guidance of the Holy Spirit in the first place. When we begin to learn how to discern the leading of the Holy Spirit, we can make right decisions and save valuable time along with resources. Remember the only decision that can be counted on to be successful in the long run are those that include choosing the route the Holy Spirit leads you to take in life. Every other choice or plan will eventually fail in due time when it is not from God.

CHAPTER 10
The Holy Spirit Will Guide Your Steps

While in prayer one morning to discern what the Holy Spirit wanted me to write about, I discerned an impression from Him. I sensed the Holy Spirit was saying to me, "A good man's steps are ordered by the Lord, and he delights in His way". I immediately knew that the Holy Spirit wanted me to write about how God directs our footsteps in life in ways we could never comprehend. God directs our steps often unknowingly in the everyday course of events. It was years after I was saved that I begin to really take a more serious developmental role in my spiritual relationship with God. Now, don't get me wrong, I was always personally aware of my walk with the Lord, but for so long I found myself in a maze of confusion and doubt. There was no roadmap in how to walk by faith, except the biblical lessons found in the Bible of course and the treasured testimonies of seasoned saints that I met in my spiritual journey. I truly did not know what the Lord wanted me to do with my life. Even though I was called to preach the gospel at the age of nineteen, I was sort of clueless on how to obtain the prophetic promises of God for my life.

There was the time when as an undergraduate student at Morehouse College, that the Lord told me that one day I would be an evangelist, but other than that particular time. I didn't know how or when that promise from God was going to come to pass in my life. I transferred from being a political science major to the religion department in my school in the hopes of getting on track regarding my call to ministry. Abandoning my lifelong dream of becoming a corporate attorney to pursue the call of God upon my life was rather easy. However, I still didn't have any clear direction. I did the only thing that I knew was the right thing at the time, I attended my classes, lived life, preached the gospel, and went to church to hear God speak to me through the sermons. Looking back upon those days now, it's evident that the Holy Spirit was directing my footsteps without me even knowing at certain times. Whether it was the janitor at Morehouse College who used to let me come into the cafeteria to have the leftovers when I didn't have any money or the times when I would walk into a church hearing God speak to me concerning a pressing situation in my life at, or receiving money from the least likely of sources when I was unemployed, the Holy Spirit had a clear way of leading my footsteps as He will do yours even when you think you are doing your own leading at the time.

You have to learn how to walk by faith when walking daily with the Holy Spirit. Walking by faith consists of you simply trusting that the Holy Spirit has your best interest in mind and that He has a specific plan for your life whether you and feel, see, or experience the specific promises of God for your life in that present moment. There will be times when you don't know what to do or which way to turn. You have to go about your daily business and know that everyday His hand is providentially guiding you to His intended destination for your life even when you can't see things unfolding in front for you. This is what makes the Christian journey a complete walk of faith and mystery.

It was years later in my walk with the Holy Spirit that I begin to recognize God's voice and how to discern his hand at times in the everyday events of my life. One day I asked God a question that revolutionized my faith in Him. I asked Him, "Do you speak to me every day?" Weeks passed by and I had forgotten about the question. Suddenly, it came to my spirit one day that our relationship with Him should be compared to our natural relationship with our earthly parents. What caring parent walks in the house after a long day at work and never even acknowledges their child. A loving, caring parent will question their child about what went on at school that day and if there is any homework that needs to be completed. If the child faced a problem at school, that parent immediately begins to offer advice. If there is a homework problem that needs to be looked at, that the child cannot understand, that parent will take the time to show their son or daughter how to work the problem step by step. After all the work has been completed, that parent will make sure to provide something to eat, all the while talking to the child before they are made to go to sleep.

There may be breaks in between the communication of the child and the parent, but for most, there is a culture of relationship between the parent and child. The following day, the parent speaks to the child before they go to school. Now when the parent goes to work, there is a break in communication until they return home again the following day. There may even be a text sent from the parent to the child instructing them to ride the bus or wait in the front of the school. So just like natural parents lend a hand in guidance and instruction, the Holy Spirit, who is the Holy Spirit of God our Father, does the same thing with us if we are whether we seem willing to listen and obey His instruction and guidance or not.

The one problem that I've noticed many Christians have is identifying when He is guiding and leading us. There are times when it is obvious and at times not so clear. One of the things I found out a while ago, is that many moves and directions that we take in life are because the Holy Spirit is actually leading us, and we don't even notice it. Have you ever decided to leave the house to run a few errands and you ran into someone that you had been thinking about over the last few days? This is more than a mere coincidence. This was the leading of the Holy Spirit of God. For example, one Monday afternoon, I was walking down the hallway of my grandmother's house and had a strong urge from the Holy Spirit that was leading me to call a childhood friend of mine. I knew immediately that it was the Holy Spirit that laid this burden on my heart to call him. I thought it was kind of strange at the time. Nevertheless, I put it off for the moment and figured I would call him in few minutes. Those few minutes added up to a couple hours and I still put off making the phone call.

Two days later, I received the news that he was involved in an altercation at his house and he ended up shooting someone. The word was that he had killed the guy. By the weekend, the story was that the young man my childhood friend had shot survived the shooting, but was severely paralyzed. Still to this day, I can't help but think if the Holy Spirit had a message that he wanted me to give my friend that could have prevented the shooting. Or was it a call to intercede in fervent prayer for my friend? We have to be honest with ourselves. There probably have been numerous occasions when the Holy Spirit was trying to direct your steps and harness your attention to something critical in importance, but you failed to obey Him or was just too busy to slow down to listen to His voice. The Holy Spirit does not shout when He is speaking, nor does He holler at us. The Holy Spirit usually speaks to us in a small still voice, through scripture, an inward witness, impacts our emotions to steer us in a certain direction, or prompts us gently when guiding us.

CHAPTER 11
Positioning Yourself To Hear The Holy Spirit

The first key to drawing closer to the Holy Spirit and hearing His voice is that you must have a personal burning desire from within. I can vividly remember those days in college when I would rush into my dorm room to play worship music and pray for hours until I would weep uncontrollably. My seat would be wet from the tears that streamed down my face. I just wanted to know God and be as close as possible to Him.

Do you really want to grow in intimacy with the Holy Spirit? The most pivotal step you can take is positioning yourself to hear from Him. God speaks to everyone in different ways. This may sound strange, but at times the Lord will speak symbolically to me by using numbers. I was born on January 22 and sometimes, I find that the Lord will use the numbers 22 or 2, to communicate to me or to confirm a message. One of the greatest lessons I learned from walking with God is that He rewards those who have a desire to hear and know Him in a greater measure than do currently.

One of the most vital things you must do is to assume a proper positioning to draw closer to the Holy Spirit in your heart. Most of the time I found myself so busy with work, family duties, and personal responsibilities that I would often lose focus on doing what it takes to hear the small still voice of the Holy Spirit. Our personal obligations, work schedule, and family can take so much of our time that, if we are not careful, our hearts will begin to become burdened and overextended with any activity other than clearing our hearts in preparation to seek the face of God. Once you make it a priority to position your heart to draw close to God, make it a point to record the numerous God encounters you experience.

Next, we must intentionally set aside time to position ourselves physically to seek the Lord in prayer. This takes focus and mental discipline because we live among a national culture in which everything is so fast paced. Start off, by selecting a place to commune with Him. When I wake up in the morning, I usually just lay still and try to quietly wait on the voice of the Holy Spirit. Other times, I might drink a cup of coffee while standing in the backyard, carefully paying attention to the sights and sounds of His creation. I ask the Holy Spirit to speak to me while I am alone in the backyard. Sometimes, He gives me an impression of a situation that I will face at work - an inner feeling of caution for the day, or a word may come to my mind that may not make sense until the day unravels. For example, there was a time the Spirit said, "Walkthrough". As an educator in the inner city, the administrators are required to do a walkthrough in my room to evaluate my progress with the students. He allows me to know of these events so when I go to work, I am mentally prepared and already abreast of what is about to happen.

Often times, the Holy Spirit speaks to me in the backyard when everyone is asleep and there is not a lot of traffic or noise in the neighborhood. Sometimes, the Holy Spirit speaks to me once I re-enter the house and begin to prepare for work. Many times, our biggest mistake is that we fail to take the time to slow down and dialogue with the Holy Spirit. He is attempting to communicate with us, but we fail to perceive the voice of God because we become so consumed with the cares of life - schoolwork, bills, duties at work, personal problems, distractions that cause us to miss God speaking to us. Job said it best in the Old Testament, "God speaks once, twice, but man perceives it not.".

God is talking to us all the time but are we really trying to listen to His voice? What if God is trying to give you the cure for cancer that could revolutionize the medical world and save the lifespan of millions of people? Due to the fact you are too busy worrying about your relationship, the distraction will cause you to miss the voice of the Holy Spirit. God has been showing you how to solve your financial problem or mental struggle, but because you haven't taken the time to slow down to hear His Holy Spirit, you will struggle in whatever problem that you are currently facing until you learn how to position yourself to come closer to the Him. You don't have to continue to find yourself in financial debt and living paycheck to paycheck. The new relationship that you in find yourself in, God already knows the final outcome. Why not take the time to ask the Holy Spirit is this is the person God is calling you to marry? You will notice that as soon as you begin to position to draw closer to God, you will receive the answers you have always needed for any life situation. I wish someone would have personally mentored me and explained to me that every decision I make requires a consult with the Holy Spirit.

Another spiritual strategy you can use to cultivate an intimate walk with the Lord is to have consistent Bible devotion every day. This requires a discipline from you and it shouldn't be rushed either. Pick a time when it is likely to be uninterrupted for communing with God in prayer while you read the Word of God. I've found out that the morning and late-night hours are some of the best times to commune with the Lord without distractions. You will notice the increased ability to hear the voice of the Holy Spirit and your ability to recognize Him talking to you in the pages of the Word. It's during these times when you find less distractions and everything is calm and settled around you. As you read your bible, you should pray and ask God for direction about what He desires you to read. The Spirit of God will lead you and reveal what He desires for you to read at that time. It may take you skimming the pages of the bible for twenty minutes, before God leads you to a particular passage of scripture, a story, or a parable that He wants you to ponder.

Sometimes God may just allow one word to jump off of the page to speak to you. I remember the time when I was staying at a relative's house and I was walking out of the kitchen. I noticed out of the corner of my eye, something small run under the cabinet by the sink. I figured that it was a mouse. Well after a few days of laying traps, and the clever mouse playing hide and go seek. I was watching television in my room, when I say a flash of gray from the side of my eye run from my under my dresser and into my closet. Well a few days later, I was reading my bible and before I closed it, it flipped by divine providence to Leviticus 11:29, which states, "Now these are to you unclean among the swarming things which swarm on the earth: the mole, AND THE MOUSE.." You see, that was God's funny way of telling me that in spite of me not being able to see the mouse fully. I was dealing with a mouse in the house. God is interested in every detail of our life, even the mouse that may be hiding in our house.

You will find the more you sacrifice time in devotion with the Lord, the more sensitive you will be to the voice of the Holy Spirit. It takes sacrifice and a willingness to draw closer to God. The most frequent seasons of deep visitations from God have been when I would awaken at five in the morning and sought out the Lord until seven. I would do only four things during this season a few years ago, read my bible, meditate on scriptures, pray, or just wait on God to speak to me. Sometimes, I did all four, just so I could draw closer to His presence.

I did this regularly for months, until I was distracted by a woman that I allowed to enter into my life. You see when you desire to get closer to the Holy Spirit, you must be on guard because Satan will send attacks, snares, and traps your way to hinder your progress in God. During this season of intense devotion, He was beginning to heal broken pieces in my life, all the while opening my ears to the voice of the Holy Spirit like never before. There were two separate occasions during this time of intense devotion that I shall never forget. I went into the grocery store to get a money order and I heard the voice of the Holy Spirit, clearly give me the name of the young woman that was standing next to me in line. There was another time that I was ministering at a youth service one Sunday, at a church in Duncanville, Texas, right outside of Dallas. Right after I stopped preaching, I heard the voice of the Holy Spirit reveal to me the name of a young man I did not know at all. I knew it was the voice of the Holy Spirit, but this was the first time I heard the Holy Spirit reveal the name of a person to me while I preached at a church. While the pastor of the church was giving the alter call, I was sitting by his wife and a few other ladies on the front row. Suddenly it happened again, the Holy Spirit spoke to me the name of a young woman I had never met before. I quietly leaned over to speak to the pastor's wife and ask her in confidentiality about the two names the Holy Spirit had revealed to me. I was shock when she told me that the woman's name was hers and she was going to the doctor the following day to get an MRI done. The name of the young man whose name was revealed by the Spirit of God, was a drummer that had left the church to go back into the world. I prayed for the pastor's wife and for the young man, interceding for the hand of the Lord to be with him in his backslidden state and divine healing for the pastor's wife.

When you make up your mind to devote more time to the Lord, you will find yourself extremely sensitive to the voice of God. There is a pattern I want to teach you about the Holy Spirit. You will never know when He will direct you to do something unexpectedly, give a warning, or even speak. When the Holy Spirit speaks, just know that it is for a purpose. God never speaks just to have idle conversation with His children. He always speaks with a divine purpose in mind that we sometimes cannot wrap our mind around at the time. You don't have to understand all the time. Often times we have the right motives in wanting to do what is right, but with so many voices in the world we live in, it is easy to be lured into the distractions.

We have to be very careful to know what voice to listen to. We should make it a habitual practice of seeking God every time there is a major decision to make in our life. If you are like me, there are many decisions that have caused me to retreat in life to find an isolated place to pray and fast for clear direction and strength. I find myself still suffering the consequences years after the actions of my twenties. You can avoid this by positioning yourself to seek clarity and divine direction when making decisions that will impact your life. This is one of the things that we must always keep in the forefront of our minds. One wrong decision can alter the course of our life forever. Don't take chances making guesses regarding pivotal choices in your life, instead sit at the feet of our Lord and hear His wisdom.

Everything that we anticipate in this life that we need an answer about should be taken before the lord in consistent and faith filled prayer. I have a desire to see many Christians, especially newcomers to the faith, begin to apply these practical spiritual principles so that their walk with the Holy Spirit will be less complicated and without hindrance, in the pursuit of their call, dreams, goals, and destiny. The bible states in Proverbs 14:12, "there is a path before each person that seems right, but in ends in death." How many people have you witnessed or heard of that took the wrong path and it led to an early death, Bankruptcy, detours, and lack of productivity? Wasting years and financial aid in college taking the wrong major because god was never sought. Decades lost never to return working on a job that doesn't bring any happiness nor fulfillment can be easily avoided. What path are you currently walking? Is this the path you've chosen or the Holy Spirit? Your current boyfriend, is it the will of God or your personal agenda? Let us allow the Holy Spirit to guide us every step along the way into our personal destiny that is awaiting our arrival.

CHAPTER 12
The Holy Spirit Speaks By Giving Impressions

When you begin to challenge your energies to spending more time with the Holy Spirit you will find that your yourself receiving impressions in your mind, heart, and inner spirit. We will also sense the peace and strength you always desired, to face all of life's uncertainties and setbacks that are sure to come our way. This is when you will find at unexpected times impressions from God out of nowhere. The Holy Spirit at time speaks not only in a gentle whisper but an impression upon your mind as well. An impression could come in the form of a picture in the mind or a thought that arises in your spirit. Trust in time that this is the Holy Spirit. This communication from the Holy Spirit comes at random times. His communication in the form of an impression often is very subtle and develops like a flash. I found with personal experience and time that the impressions of the Holy Spirit come, when

I'm usually engaged in some type of random activity like cleaning the house or laying quietly on my bed.

An impression from the Holy Spirit, supernaturally gives us detailed information we would have not know otherwise. For example, my mother's side of the family always has a family reunion every two years in the first week of August. This particular family reunion, I left a day earlier to take care some personal business. While lying down in my bedroom in silence, I had an impression from the Holy Spirit of my oldest daughter Camille. The picture that formed in my mind seemed to be as if she fell backward into a pool of water. The next day when I was asking Camille did she enjoy herself at the family reunion. The first thing out of her mouth was, "Daddy, I almost drowned!" As I thought for a second, the Holy Spirit immediately reminded me of the impression I had received, just the day before in my duplex apartment. This was a new beginning for me of discerning of how the Spirit of the Lord can speak to us if we are willing to listen and have a heart to want to know the voice of God.

I vividly remember another time; I was laying on a blowup mattress during the morning time before heading off to work. I had an impression of three young girls that were students in my sixth-grade class at the time. I immediately recognized the faces of all three of the girls faces. I sensed immediately sensed in my spirit, that I needed to be on guard at work while in the classroom later on and sensitive to what the Holy Spirit was trying to show me. In my spirit, I had the feeling that these three young ladies were up to no good, but I just couldn't put my finger on it. Half way through the school day, the school counselor made a visit to my classroom. This was out of the ordinary because she never came to visit me in my classroom. We usually spoke casually while passing each other in the hallways or in school meetings. She informed that these three young girls were attempting to get me in trouble by accusing me of being unfair in my discipline practice in the classroom toward them. Not only did they accuse me of this but their female science teacher as well. I wasn't even surprised at the words of the counselor, except for the young black girl that the Holy Spirit showed me who was a part of the complaint. I had really gone above and beyond the norm to reach out to her and challenge her academically in the classroom. The other two ladies it was not really a huge surprise for me at all, since they had been giving me discipline problems in the classroom, by begin rude and distrustful in the classroom for the past couple of months. If we are willing to listen to even the little impressions that come to our mind and not disregard them. We will find ourselves two steps ahead of anything Satan may try to throw our way.

An impression can come in a variety of ways, but the two dominate methods are pictures in the mind and flashes of thoughts or revelation within your inner spirit. There have been times when unexpectedly, the Holy Spirit would bring a picture to my mind, so I begin to carry a journal around with throughout the day and place it by my bedside at night just in case I received a revelation from the Spirit in the form of a picture impression, I would be able to immediately write it down, so that I wouldn't forget it. Always remember, that any time God decides to speak, there is a divine purpose and reason behind it. He doesn't speak, just to hold idle conversation, as we humans normally tend to do. There is always a significant purpose whenever the Lord chooses to communicate with us.

Another way, the Holy Spirit, uses impressions to communicate to us is by often flashing a revelation or inner knowing within our spirit. Some people have spoken about having a nervous feeling come into their stomach when something seemed to be wrong or there was danger lurking. I've experienced that feeling as well whenever the Lord is preparing me for an encounter from the enemy, verbal attack, or situation that He is trying to steer me away from. The more time you spend walking with the Lord the more you will begin to be aware of the impressions you receive from the Holy Spirit as they come to you. We must remember that the Spirit of the Lord always deals with people in unique ways. He knows best how to reach everyone.

There will be times when you may meet someone for the first time, and something within you tells you not to cautious about them. That is an impression from the Holy

Spirit giving you a warning within your inner spirit. You've more than likely experienced this feeling before and just couldn't put a finger on what it was. Have you ever been in a particular place and just felt the need to leave that place for some strange reason and you couldn't articulate at that present moment? You may have thought about it as just a gut feeling. Maybe your friends didn't even understand why you were leaving. You probably did not understand it either at the time. We may never know why God gives us certain impressions. Just rest in the knowledge that our all-seeing God sees all. Nothing is hidden from His eyes, especially not the unexpected danger and satanic traps laid in our path. Somethings we will never be able to understand until we see Him face to face in heaven.

One time a close friend and I were headed to a club in my hometown over our summer break from college. As he was driving down the street on the way to the club, suddenly I felt an eerie feeling come all over me. It was as if I was nervous. My stomach was uneasy. We were seven minutes away from the club, but I just couldn't shake this strange impression for one reason or another. I sat quietly in the passenger seat, listening to the music and making small talk trying to catch up on old times. Suddenly, we drove up alongside the scene of a crash. The smoke was filtering from the engine of one of the cars and there was a crowd of people standing on the side of the road. As we inched by the wrecked cars in our automobile, it was evident from an inner impression within that someone was dead. I looked over to who was to become my best friend as he stared in silence at the wreckage and asked him one question. "Did you feel the spirit of death?" He turned his shoulders and face toward me and said, "I did!' Without exchanging another word, we knew that according to the timing of the wreck, we could have been the ones who had died that night because we had started out of the house about ten to fifteen minutes late (as usual). Be aware of the impressions of the Holy Spirit, they could possibly save your life.

I remember dating a young lady that I had met in college. After a few months of dating, one day I turned around to face her while in the midst of an argument and simply told her that I didn't trust her. Unfortunately, time would reveal why I felt the way I did. You don't have to wrestle with the notion that the Holy Spirit is trying to protect us not only from situations but people who don't have the right intentions and motives. He knows everything about the people that we interact with… more than we could ever possibly perceive.

Positioning ourselves to hear from the Lord helps us recognize the impressions that come from the Holy Spirit. Meditation, prayer, and studying the Word of God makes us more sensitive to the impressions that come from God in over time. I have noticed that an impression from the Holy Spirit is sometimes a very subtle knowing that comes to our inner spirit. That's why it's necessary to sit intentionally and be quiet for a moment to allow the Spirit of the Lord time to minister to us as He so chooses. I often found out that impressions come at the least likely of times when we least expect it. Start making a habit of turning your radio off while commuting to work or just cleaning your house without any televisions or music playing in the background. Begin to ask the Holy Spirit to speak you by giving you an impression of maybe something you need to do that day, an innovative idea, solution to a relationship crisis, or someone you need to call that He may lead you to that needs a word of encouragement. You must be willing to be open and receptive to the pictures that may come to your mind or intuitive feelings that rise up within your spirit. Don't avoid these signs from the Holy Spirit because He is trying to talk to you.

One of the things that you must always keep in mind is that God loves His children and wants the best for them. Have you ever driven down the same street for years and immediately noticed things that seem to be out of the ordinary? Maybe you have driven that street for years and then all of a sudden you see something that would not have been as obvious such as a sign or new neighbors to someone that was unfamiliar with the neighborhood. You were able to immediately recognize what was new because you had grown accustomed to seeing the same sights and landmarks. That's the same thing when it comes the foresight of God when it pertains to our personal life. He sees everything out of place that we need to be aware of before we even have a chance to realize what is out of the ordinary. The Lord has the sovereign ability to know everything and see everything before it even comes into existence. It is vital that we learn to walk with the Holy Spirit and play very close attention to the impressions that He gives us. If you take the time to be silent and just allow the Holy Spirit to bring to your mind the many times that you had a gut feeling not to do something and you failed to do it, you will find that you usually regret doing the exact opposite of what you felt led in your inner spirit to do. Make it a conscious effort from here on out, to be sensitive to the inner impression within your spirit and the sudden images that come to your mind. It could just save your life.

CHAPTER 13
Prompts From The Holy Spirit

Definition of a prompt - (A) to move to action, (B) to assist by suggesting or saying the next words of something forgotten or imperfectly learned.

Another lesson that the Holy Spirit is willing to impart unto you is His communication by the method of prompting. The notable part about this type of communication from the Holy Spirit is that it comes to us often without words. While a lot like an impression, it is different in that it comes often without the sense of urgency.

Becoming skilled at discerning and recognizing the prompting of the Holy Spirit takes time. It is a spiritual discipline that cannot be learned overnight. What took years of frustrating trial and error for me, can take you just a few months if you learn how to train your spirit correctly. One of the most significant insights about being led by the Holy Spirit is grasping the understanding that He is versatile in the way that He talks to us. The Lord speaks to each of us in diverse manners throughout the course of our day. One minute the Holy Spirit will try to relay a message through a specific scripture in the Bible, while a few hours later, you may hear the soft whisper of His voice. Then, sometimes, the Spirit of the Lord may just direct you concerning a personal matter by giving you a prompt.

Let me give you a modern-day perfect analogy of how prompts from the Holy Spirit work. Have you ever watched an awards show on television such as the VMA or Grammy Awards? If you will notice carefully, the celebrities are looking forward into the television camera reading from something that is hidden from the viewers sight. Even though you see can't what they are reading from, you know something is present. Every sentence and highlight of the show is already written and the only thing the presenter needs to do is follow the script from the teleprompter. An effective life for the Christian at times is just like being on stage and being dependent on a teleprompter for every move, sentence, and comment. Even in the old days, television sitcoms that were taped in front of audiences used signs with words to guide the actors through there acting scenes on stage. The stage crew would have things written on poster boards to direct the actors in what to do or say next. The poster boards were used to give a sense of personal direction for the actors throughout the television show. Those seated in the audience can witness everything that's going on if they are close enough to the stage. Why are the celebrities given the words to say from the teleprompter? The presenters may not truly know the fellow celebrity that they are about to introduce to the stage. So, to make things run smoothly, the celebrities are given the precise words to say to ensure that the award show runs smoothly. To make the impact in the culture in which we live as Christians, we must be willing to follow the exact directions of the prompts of the Holy Spirit. The Holy Spirit is type of teleprompter when we find ourselves facing certain people, situations, problems, or crossroads in our life. The Holy Spirit will give us a prompt or a nudge in the right direction to follow the right path in which to travel.

My first year of teaching in the public-school system in Fort Worth as an English teacher was a trying year. I can remember when we had a department meeting one afternoon after school. I sat by in the school's cafeteria as a group of teachers were voicing their complaints about the school's new administration. It was as if everyone was going around the circle, voicing their dislikes and complaints about what the schools administration was doing and what they needed to do to run the school more effectively. Right before it was my turn as the new teacher to speak up about how my year was going in the classroom, I felt a prompt in my spirit not to say anything negative at all regarding the school's new administration. It wasn't a voice I heard. It was just a gentle nudge within me to remain quiet from voicing any complaints along with the other educators. This wasn't the time to find a scripture to see if what I was sensing was from the Lord. I just had a knowing from the inside of me that the Lord was telling me to not say anything negative regarding the school's administration. I totally disregarded that prompting from the Holy Spirit and just begin to spew out my lists of complaints and concerns without any constraints. Oh God, why did I do that? It didn't take long for me to find out after that meeting that somethings are just better left unsaid. A few days later after the meeting the vice principal and I had a few well selected exchanges of words regarding another matter. Indirectly, she informed me that she knew of the words that I had shared with my fellow colleagues that particular afternoon when I disregarded the prompt from the Spirit to refrain from engaging in negative talk before the faculty meeting. Nothing I said was inappropriate. In fact, it was the truth. However, there was a lesson to be learned and I learned it immediately following that conversation. Being obedient to the prompting of the Holy Spirit is more important that following your personal emotions.

Promptings from the Holy Spirit give us immediate direction that nine times out of ten would not have taken place if we would have relied on our own actions. The prompts when obeyed, allow things to flow more smoothly in the course of our life. A valuable life lesson I learned regarding prompts from God is that when they come, there is no time to second guess that you received direction from Him. There have often been times when I sensed a prompting from Him, only to override the feeling or eventually talk myself out of believing that I just received a prompt. It seems to me that when a prompt comes, it often brings a certain inner awareness and personal understanding within that God has just communicated with you in His own mysterious sort of way.

I shall never forget the time I was in church one afternoon all alone praying for personal things I was believing for at the time and interceding for others. I was preparing to turn off the lights in the church and leave to go home but I was prompted to take oil and pray over the entire facility, especially over the doors of the church. I took the oil from behind the pulpit and begin to spread oil over the doors of the church and pray. After twenty minutes of praying, I locked the doors behind me and drove home. The following day, I walked into the church to follow my normal routine of personal prayer in solitude without any interruption. When I walked into the side entrance of the church, the very first things that I noticed was that the side entrance door was wide open. I don't know how long the door had been opened, but as I walked around the church sanctuary and property. The amazing fact that stood out was that there was nothing missing from the church property. The side entrance door was positioned on a street in the community that was very peculiar. I was astonished that no one stole any of the recording equipment, instruments, chairs, etc. from the facility. When I looked around in silence, the Holy Spirit reminded me of the prompt from Him just a day ago to pray over the doors of the church. It may not always make sense to obey a prompt from the Holy Spirit, but it pays off in the end.

CHAPTER 14
How The Holy Spirit Gives Inner Conviction

One of the things that I have come to realize the most about the Holy Spirit, is that He wants the best for His children. Sometimes, this means telling us when we are absolutely dead wrong in a matter. I remember my grandmother telling me while we were in her bedroom one evening, "I wouldn't want to serve a God that jumps every time we ask him to do something. We treat God as if He is a Las Vegas slot machine!" We automatically assume sometimes in our life, due to our selfishness and self-centered pride, that God's job is to give us what want we all the time. As time passes by, we should begin to mature in our understanding of God and recognize that our relationship with Him is just like our relationships with others in our family and friendships. It's a give and take relationship. So many times, we find ourselves mainly on the taking end of our spiritual relationship with our

Heavenly Father. This is when the Holy Spirit comes in to convict us of our personal sin, wrong attitudes, and ungodly issues in our life that need to be properly dealt with in a timely manner if we expect to keep an open line of communication open with Heaven.

The Holy Spirit loves us too much to see us live our lives below our divine potential in Him. So, every now and then, God will shake us in certain areas to get our attention so we can see the things that are displeasing in His sight. When we sin intentionally or unintentionally, we find ourselves quenching the Holy Spirit. The word quench in the Greek means to extinguish, make stop, or put out something. Sin in the life of a believer quenches or hinders the presence of the Lord in our life. Without the presence of the Holy Spirit, we will soon find ourselves drying up spiritually and operating in our own personal human strength. This eventually will breed inner frustration and failure in life in due time. The apostle Paul said that we should be filled with the Spirit (Eph. 5:18). The baptism of the Holy Spirit is a one-time experience that happens in the life of the believer as they accept Christ.

When we allow sin, wrong motives, negative attitudes, and ungodly choices to enter into our personal life. It will eventually begin to suppress the move of the Holy Spirit in our life. When this happens and the Spirit is suppressed, if we are not careful, we will find ourselves in a dangerous state of sliding back from the things of God. The only other state worse off than being backslidden is not experiencing eternal salvation. When you begin to feel, sense, and hear less of the Holy Spirit in your life, and you are not as connected with the Lord as in times past. You will often notice, that the Holy Spirit will begin to or has already convicted you about things in your life such as sin, wrong relationships, negative thinking, and even letting go of past hurts. One of the things that I've noticed in my personal walk over these past fourteen years is that when you bring a complaint to the Lord in regard to someone else or a group of people, you have felt have sinned against you, He will often deal first with your personal life and heart, before even addressing the very concern that you brought before Him in prayer. Why is this so at times? God is more interested in our character and personal relationship with Him than our personal feelings regarding a matter at times. He will take care of the wrongs that have been done toward you, because He is the final judge.

When the Holy Spirit convicts you, it's often because God is trying to get your attention in regard to something that displeases Him and wants you to change. God does not get the glory in our life when we are slaves to sin or habitually doing things that have the potential to destroy our integrity, family, health, finances, and destiny. So, every now and then, when we find ourselves steering off the path of righteousness, the Holy Spirit will convict us of something that we need to address or let go in our personal life. I'll never forget the time, over a decade ago, I was visiting family members in Houston, Texas for Thanksgiving. We had all gathered up at my uncle's house to celebrate the holiday. My oldest daughter was not even a year old at the time and her mother and I had gone through a divorce that left us with feelings of animosity and bitterness toward one another. The Lord used my grandmother and mother as instruments to speak to me about letting go of the past and asking God for the strength to let go of the feelings of anger I had allowed to build up toward her about the things that had been done and the words spoken against me. I was instantly convicted by the Holy Spirit as they both spoke to me with concern. I walked outside and asked God to free me from the anger that was pinned up on the inside of me for the past year. I felt as if ten thousand pounds of brick had been immediately lifted from my shoulders as soon as I asked God to remove the anger in my life. All I could do was weep uncontrollably in the front yard of my uncle's townhouse. Before that burden was removed from my life, I was just beginning my walk as a new Christian, but I knew deep on the inside of me that the Lord was dealing with me concerning my anger. You see that anger wasn't going to destroy her, but it would me in the long run if I left it unchecked. God's omniscience is evident in the ability to foresee the danger and the pitfalls ahead of us and it often moves Him to convict us so that we can deal with the areas of our life that need to change so that we can continue to grow in Him unhindered.

Jesus said in John 16:8, "And when He comes, He will convict the world in regard to sin." There are times when our actions and lifestyle force the Holy Spirit to convict us regarding the sin in our life, the conditions of our hearts, disobedience to His known revealed will, or even just the way we treat people. Imagine that you do something that grieves your mother, such as lying to her about your grades in college or committing a crime that will require you to spend time in prison for a couple of years. This would cause your mother to grieve naturally and would impact your relationship in a negative manner with her. This is the exact same thing that happens with us when we do things that the Holy Spirit observes that are not pleasing in His sight. I've made many mistakes during my life that have personally convicted me - wrong thinking, actions of rebellion, and errors that will never be wiped away. During these frustrating and rebellious years of my life, my own mother was naturally grieved because she didn't raise me to run the streets, smoke weed, get drunk, or hang out with the guys in the neighborhood. My acts of foolishness and immaturity caused my mother to suffer greatly.

I shall never forget the time when I came home drunk barely able to step out of the car one Saturday night while hanging out with my cousins. My youngest cousin had just been murdered along with her boyfriend in north Dallas and I was suffering severely on the inside. Even though God prepared me for her death nearly six months before she was murdered, I was still hurting and in shock like so many of my family members. I still had to deal with the feelings of shock and of losing someone in such a tragic manner that I had grown up with as a child. All that night the only thing I could do was reminisce on the last time I had spoken with her inside of the nightclub in North Dallas that she was too young to be in, in the first place. Before I could step out the car and stumble up the driveway to the back of the house that night, my eyes locked with my mother's eyes. All I could see was disappointment, worry, and concern. I knew my mother had raised me better than this, but I had taken a wrong road. Her grief disconnected us for a few days. We barely spoke to one another and when we did, it was not even two sentences long in comment and reply on both of our ends. It was quite obvious that she was feeling heavy in her spirit wondering what had become of her only son. I imagine this is exactly how our relationship with the Holy Spirit is when engage in sin. The sin of pornography, lying, deceit, alcoholism, adultery, pride, fits of rage, racism, envy, jealousy, gossip, and even deception grieves Him. The main objective of the Holy Spirit in convicting us is to always turn us back to Him. He desires to turn us away from the sin that is in the process of destroying our life, to connect us back to a right relationship with God, and to help identify areas in our life that we need to deal with so that we become more effective Christians.

Growth in your relationship with the Holy Spirit, depends on your ability to humbly accept the conviction

He highlights in your life. You must be willing to not only accept and submit to the conviction of the Holy Spirit but more importantly know that the areas He highlights that need correction are things He feels will limit your potential.

There are myriad of ways in which the Holy Spirit brings conviction. Sometimes He will use scripture to show us about areas that need to be corrected or an inner witness. Other times, He will communicate by way of a dream, vision, or through the conversation of another believer in Christ. There will be times that He will use someone else that is close to you to convict you to get your attention. After King David set up Bathsheba's husband Uriah in the frontline of the battle to be assassinated, the Prophet Nathan was responsible for confronting King David with his sins which led to David's personal conviction. There will be times when God will use someone in your life that is close to you to convict you of personal sin. If you harden your heart regarding the sin in your life, the Holy Spirit will not hesitate to address the sin in your life by sending someone to confront you face to face. That's why even though we as Christians are mortal human beings and will engage in sinful practices, we should try our hardest never to find ourselves comfortable with the sin in our life. If we keep putting off dealing with what the Holy Spirit is trying to convict us of, God will expose us so that we see the path we are heading down is toward destruction. Trust me. He will do it!

CHAPTER 15
The Holy Spirit And Supernatural Events

There are stories spread throughout the Bible that give us insight into how the Holy Spirit overtly presents Himself at times in supernatural ways. Have you ever read about the story of Philip in the Book of Acts (Acts 8:26-40) and how the Spirit of the Lord, carried him away from the Ethiopian eunuch that was sitting in the carriage, as he began to walk away? As I ponder the story of Philip the Evangelist being supernaturally transported from the location of the Ethiopian eunuch, I can't but help to think about the times the Holy Spirit has mysteriously acted in our lives sometimes without us knowing. Many biblical scholars would argue that this was a one-time event that took place in the Bible and that certain scenarios such as the one with Philip, The Evangelist, do not occur today.

Let's evaluate the account. Philip was an evangelist of

the gospel who being well versed and knowledgeable of the scriptures, God, made a divine appointment to cross paths with the Ethiopian eunuch who was a ranking member of his government's treasury department. He was directed by the Angel of the Lord, to "Go south to the road - the desert road - that goes down from Jerusalem to Gaza." He found himself at the carriage of a eunuch who was an Ethiopian governmental leader who was interested in the understanding of the scriptures he was reading in a more clear and understandable manner. After Philip explained the scriptures in its entirety, and Ethiopian treasury leader desired to be baptized. The scriptures indicate, in Acts 8:39, "When they came out of the water, the Spirit of the Lord suddenly took Philip away." Does thing type of strange phenomena still take place today on the earth?

During my junior year of college, I was on fire for God. Except for the occasional beer on the weekend, I had a heart to do the will of the Father at all cost. I remember running into an older Caucasian lady one day, after picking up some money that my mother wired me. She came off almost like a vagabond, with a van in her possession that stood out because it was stacked to the ceiling with household goods, clothes, and old worn books. I can't even remember how we started talking to one another, but the conversation immediately turned into a discussion about God. Toward the end of the conversation, she invited me to over to her house to continue our discussion about God and the spiritual life in more detail. Before departing from the retail store, I took down her number and promised to call her in a few days. A few days eventually turned into a week due to my collegiate studies and activities on campus. This older Caucasian lady and me – a much younger African American college junior had finally arranged for me to come to her house for an evening during the next week after class.

I didn't know the exact location where she stayed but I knew it was in walking distance from the school campus. That afternoon before departing, I asked a college buddy of mine if he didn't mind accompanying me on the walk to the lady's house. He agreed and we left out later that afternoon to make the trip. I already knew that the address that she gave me was at least a fifteen-minute walk from the college campus. And I also knew that we needed to be on guard for thieves and any local stick up kids in the neighborhood. When we finally arrived, it was later in the day, around seven in the evening. After knocking briskly on the metal framed door and looking around our surroundings for a few moments. She immediately let us in and for a few hours, my friend and I, along with this older lady, discussed the Bible and the sovereignty of God in the universe. As the conversation winded down, with it being night outside, my friend and I looked at each other knowing without saying a word that it was time for us to leave. After she said a brief prayer for my friend and I to arrive safely back on campus, we proceeded to leave.

We stepped her porch of the ran down duplex and immediately, my friend and I looked at each other in a moment of silence. We needed to navigate our way back to campus quick and safely because it was night time and we heard and personally knew of many stories of college kids getting robbed at night off campus in the local community. We weren't necessarily paranoid, we just made it a point to be aware of our surroundings as we prepared ourselves to take the hike back to campus. Ten minutes into our walk back to the school campus something supernatural happened in the like manner of Philip the Evangelist from the Book of Acts. As my friend and I were walking, the Spirit of the Lord took us and supernaturally pushed us forward like Philip experienced after he got through baptizing the Ethiopian eunuch. Before we even knew it, we were a one-minute walk from the campus. Words can't even explain the experience that night. My former college buddy, last time I checked, is located in the Dallas/Fort Worth Metroplex area. He can attest to that night in Atlanta. We had a Philip experience that we both shall never forget. It was like we were transported in time and space from one location to another while walking but our speed was accelerated. We stood up all night in awe, trying to explain to ourselves what happened. I believe in my heart, that God supernaturally accelerated our speed as we were walking through the neighborhood that night by way of the Spirit of the Lord, to protect us from danger.

During the years of 2009 and 2010, the Lord spoke to me consistently through the avenue of dreams. He was giving me vivid warnings and specific revelation concerning things that were going on around me at the present time. I had never experienced anything like it before in my life. For some strange reason, God was showing me the sins of people in the community and those around me who were personally connected to me. That particular season of my life, I often have labeled the season of divine visitation. Every week, the Spirit of God was visiting me by way of a dream, vision, or supernatural experience like the prophets of old experienced in the Old Testament. I still don't understand why this season of my life consisted of so many unordinary visitations. Maybe because he knew my current situation was full of trials, spiritual struggle, and demonic attacks.

There was one particular dream from the Spirit of God that seemed to leave me in awe and shock after I awakened in the middle of night. I was experiencing so many supernatural visitations from the Lord, that it was to the point, that I kept a journal beside my bed to record my dreams so that I wouldn't forget anything. One particular night, I remember being awakened out of sleep in a cold sweat because I just couldn't believe what was revealed to me in the dream that night. I turned on the bedroom light and immediately begin writing down everything I perceived the Lord was telling me. The Lord revealed to me that someone close to me was committing adultery with someone that I knew. I asked for wisdom in how to approach the individual that was involved in the affair. One day I pulled the individual to the side and communicated to this person everything that was revealed to me in the dream that night. Not once did this person deny it. On the contrary, they admitted that everything that I said was true and walked away with their head down in silence.

I'll never forget the time I was arrested in Atlanta, Georgia for rolling through a stop sign on the campus of Clark Atlanta University. My friends and I had just walked from Auburn Avenue in downtown Atlanta to the Atlanta University Center after participating in the Auburn Festival. When the police officer took my license and ran my paperwork, he was alerted that I had an outstanding warrant for an unpaid traffic ticket I had forgotten to pay back in Texas. I had the tedious experience of spending the next three nights in the local county jail in Bankhead, right on the outskirts of downtown Atlanta. After lunch, on my second day in jail, while awaiting bond so I could finally go home, an older gentleman in his mid-forties and I struck up a conversation in the middle of the jail tank. Under the inspiration of the Holy Spirit, he suddenly began to prophesy to me right in that tank on the fourth floor of the jail. What's so profound is that he called out a secret sin that I had been dealing with for the past few years and showed me under the inspiration of the Holy Spirit what would happen if I took two specific roads in my life. One would be a life of relative comfort if I decided to obey God and follow His will for my life. Another road, he insisted would be one of addiction and homelessness. I decided that day in jail that I would attempt to live a life for God to avoid the possible destruction that lie ahead if I continued to live life on my own terms. I was astonished to say the least at this prophetic encounter that I had with this inmate. The lesson I learned that afternoon, surrounded by a majority of African-American male inmates awaiting trial and release from jail, is that God is willing to reach you even in jail after eating lunch. It doesn't matter where or when, but the Holy Spirit, loves you enough to convict you of any known or unknown sin in your life. Yes, even if it's in a jail tank, on the fourth floor awaiting bond and release.

CHAPTER 16
Be Willing To Be Led By The Spirit

The Holy Spirit of Truth is willing to lead you in your every decision whether it is in your marriage, selection of a career, purchase of a home, personal finances, and even in business investments. You need to be willing to be led! Starting today, before you leave the house or your apartment, seek the leading of the Guide. Make it a habit of asking the Holy Spirit to lead you and guide throughout the day. The Bible states in Psalm 37:23, "The steps of a good man are ordered by the Lord..." You will often find in life that the people you meet, the places you randomly visit, have a specific hidden agenda for you. It may take days or even years for you to understand this fully, but in due time, you will understand why you met the man on the street corner who needed inspiration for the day, the lady at the grocery store who gave you a word of encouragement while you were going through your very own rough patch in life.

One day while driving down through the downtown area of Ogden, Utah, I noticed a young Caucasian couple in their early twenties walking down the clean street. I felt led by the Lord, to pull over and witness to this couple. Keep in mind that at the time, I was staying in the state of Utah, the Mormon capital of the world. As I stepped out of the car and approached the young couple with quiet confidence, I simply asked them about their spiritual life and if they believed in Jesus Christ as the Savior of the entire world. They shook their heads in unison that they did not. I boldly begin to witness to them on this downtown street about their eternal need for a Savior. All I remember is what stood out to me, after I left, was that the couple informed me that no one had ever shared the gospel of Jesus Christ with them every before. To say the least, I was astonished. It was the year 2007, in the twenty first century in America, and these two Caucasian youth had never been witnessed to before regarding the Gospel of Jesus Christ. They nodded their heads for prayer. I hope that in their journey here on earth they met God as Savior for themselves.

Maybe the church in America, needs to re¬evaluate its stance on missions and evangelism. I've noticed a trend of missionary organizations and churches beginning to offer short term mission trips to the inland of the urban cities spread throughout our vast nation. Our mission as a church should be to do what Jesus commanded us to do in the Book of Acts. He gave the spiritual orders in Acts 1:8, "be my witnesses in Jerusalem, in all of Judea and Samaria, and to the ends of the earth.". To begin in Jerusalem, is the evangelistic call to first start sharing the gospel in our very own hometown before we spread out to evangelize the lost in other regions and countries of the world. All throughout the day, there are enormous amounts of people that we encounter, that need to hear our testimony, be witnessed to, given a word of inspiration, or receive prayer. Start allowing the Holy Spirit to led you to these people starting today. Be sensitive to His voice and the promptings that you receive from Him.

One of the most encouraging things I've experienced continually to help strengthen my faith in God is when I obey and follow the leading of the Holy Spirit. The outcome of my obedience always inspires me in my personal journey with the Holy Spirit. For example, it could be as simple as feeling led to call someone that He suddenly laid upon my heart. There have been times, when I decided to call the person I felt led to contact. Usually, the conversation starts with brief casual talk and finally after about five minutes I inform them that the Holy Spirit led me to call them. I will receive one of two responses, silence, or they will begin to share with me personal matters that they are currently facing.

A few summers ago I was outside in my grandmother's

backyard when the Holy Spirit showed me the face of a pastor whose church I use to attend. I hadn't talked to this particular pastor in over five months. I called him and the conversation dragged along very slow in the beginning. Initially, I was hesitant, to speak with him at first, but I informed him that the Holy Spirit, showed me an impression of his face and I wanted to be obedient to the direction of the Lord. He quietly asked me, did the Lord give me anything to share with him. As I sat on the phone fidgeting, there was complete silence on both ends of the phone. Finally, the word patience came to my mind. I shared the word patience with him and how I sensed the Lord was cultivating this fruit of the Spirit in his life during this current season. His response was simple, silence on his end. He said a few words and we both ended the conversation with a cordial but obviously distant goodbye. I thought to myself, after hanging up the phone, that it had been a very unsuccessful mission that the Holy Spirit just initiated me to engage in.

The story didn't end there. A few months later that same pastor called me to let me know that when I called him, he was going through some personal struggles in his ministry, and that one phone call from me was a sign of encouragement given to him from the Lord. You see, if you're willing to follow the direction of the Holy Spirit, even in the very small things, something as trivial as a phone call, you may never know, how the Spirit of Truth, will decide to use you to be a blessing to someone else.

CHAPTER 17
The Holy Spirit Doesn't Shout, He Simply Whispers

Definition of Whisper - to speak softly with little or no vibration of the vocal cords specifically to avoid being overheard.

One of the greatest books in my opinion, regarding how the Holy Spirit speaks in a whisper is, The Power of a Whisper, by Bill Hybel. Bill Hybel, is the founding pastor of Willow Creek Community Church, in Barrington, Illinois. Willow Creek has often been labeled, one of the most influential churches in North America. I came across, The Power of a Whisper, one day while looking for a good book to read, while scanning the aisles of Mardell's Bookstore. By the time of my discovery of this book, I was already quite familiar with hearing the whispers of the Holy Spirit. To be frank, I cannot really remember the first time I heard my first whisper from the Holy Spirit.

However, while writing this chapter, the Holy Spirit, reminded me of one of the times that stands out as a moment I shall never forget.

I hadn't been a Christian for more than two years when I heard His voice whisper to me one afternoon. I was resting from the college homecoming festivities earlier that day, and I was trying to mentally map out how the rest of the homecoming day would go. It was around 5 or 6 pm, when I distinctly heard the whisper of the Holy Spirit, give me specific instructions. The Holy Spirit whispered, "Don't leave the campus, because you are going to wreck your car!" It was no denying that I just had heard a voice! I was the only one in my dorm room at the time. The words were so precise and clear. It shocked me to my core, because I never had experienced anything like that before in my life. It was unmistakable that I just heard the voice of God, because while I was sitting on my bed, the television, laptop, and radio were all turned off. What do you do, when you just hear a voice, warn you not to drive or you will wreck your car?

I sat on my bed motionless for a few minutes. Unfortunately, I begin to think of the young lady visiting from Florida that I had just met earlier that day. I had met her earlier that day during the homecoming tailgate and we hit it off fairly well. After exchanging phone numbers, I promised to see her later that night, before she left to go home to Florida the following day. This was all before I heard the warning that came in the form of a whisper! Her cousin and I, knew each other, and had hung out a few times on and off campus together. He was a part of a fraternity that was heavily involved in social and political issues on campus. That night, after drinking and smoking marijuana all day long. I drove my car toward the frat house that was about ten minutes away from the campus, to meet up with the young lady before she left town. As I was driving, I decided to not go by the frat house, because I called the house phone, and no one picked up. I made the next available right on the next street and then it happened suddenly without any notice. Bammmm! I wrecked my car! I passed out briefly from the impact, behind the wheel, and before coming to my senses. I had run into the back of a parked car which forced the car that I hit, to hit a parked car in front of it. All I can say is the situation was very bad.

I could have lost my life or better yet killed someone that night, all because I failed to obey the whisper of the Holy Spirit. At that time, I was fairly new in my walk with God. I was doing a lot of compromising and engaging in worldly activity at the point. If I knew then what I know now, about how the Holy Spirit could whisper to you and hold a conversation with you, like what I mentioned in the previous passage, I would have probably been quicker to obey and heed His instruction from the whisper on that particular wintry afternoon. I would have never wrecked my car and could have avoided a lot of personal detours up the road. How does one learn how to cultivate a listening ear to hear the Holy Spirit, as He gives gentle directions and warnings to you? It all starts with a sincere desire and a heart to seek God in fervent prayer. The more that you pray, read the Word of God, meditate, listen to sermons, and fast, your spiritual ears will be sensitive, to discern the voice of the Spirit speaking to you in gentle nods and pressing in your inner spirit.

A whisper from the Holy Spirit is when the Holy Spirit speaks to you in a gentle manner. His whispers come in a variety of unexpected ways. It could be a simple thought, whether you hear Him from the inside of your spirit, your ears, or from a source outside of your body, such as someone speaking to you. The Spirit of the Lord often communicates in a soft audible voice, that is so precise at times, that you cannot deny that you have heard from Him. I've noticed, that when He speaks, there will be a very tranquil voice that you will sense communicating with you from out of nowhere. You must begin to recognize the personality of the Holy Spirit in your journey with Him, by recognizing His whispers in the most unexpected of places.

He is very spontaneous and cannot be predicted on certain occasions. He can show up to speak to you anytime, anywhere, and by any mode of communication, that He deems feasible to relay a message to you. It is very critical for you to understand, that if you desire, a sure way to arrive to the destiny God has been created for your life, you will have to learn how to identify when the Holy Spirit is whispering to you. There was a time when I was involved in a very rocky relationship. While engaging in prayer with my cousin who is a pastor regarding the matter, the Holy Spirit whispered, "She is intentionally trying to push you away." I immediately stopped praying and understood that the Spirit of the Lord had just given me divine information that He was aware of regarding that relationship. I didn't want to face this hard, true fact, but it was obvious that I was allowing myself to remain in a relationship that the other person was intentionally trying to sabotage while I was trying to salvage what was left of the remaining pieces. Be willing to be vulnerable and allow yourself to hear the wisdom from the whispers of God.

CHAPTER 18
The Holy Spirit Allows Us To Walk In The Supernatural

One of the things, that has always seemed to amaze me throughout the years of watching movies, is how Hollywood often produces characters in movies that have unique supernatural abilities. Every year or so, Hollywood producers create a new storyline for consumers that consist of villains and superheroes that are unordinary. Some of these supernatural humans can fly or walk on buildings. Some possess superhuman strength and others have the ability to vanish into midair. I grew up in a time when Superman and Batman were the superheroes on the silver screen. Before I graduated elementary school, the Ninja Turtles were the new superheroes that lined the shelves of major retail supermarket chains. Who would have ever imagined, that the heroes of my fifth-grade years, for most of my classmates and myself, were talking turtles that were from birth trained to be lethal ninjas in the art of karate? Let's not forget the X-Men, Iron Man, the list grows every year.

Have you ever wondered, why not Americans only? The world over is fascinated with the superheroes displayed on the movie screen. My belief, is that we as everyday people, are drawn in amazement, to people that have the ability to defy human normalcy. So often humans find themselves living their lives in ritual mundane terms without excitement or personal fulfillment. Many of us become slaves to routine, never breaking out of our normal routine schedule for twelve months, except for a one- or two-week vacation. Many of us wake up to brush our teeth, only to head to jobs that we have personal disdain for, but because we are tied financial obligations, we simply can't dismiss. This happens faithfully, Monday thru Friday. Subconsciously, whether we know it or not, we find ourselves stuck in a routine that is not only boring but limiting to our creativity. In other words, we as humans are possibly drawn to movies that portray superheroes because they embody what we have a heart to seek and find - Adventure and defiance of the odds.

Secondly, humans are attracted to the supernatural world. We as believers in Jesus Christ are a part of that world, but so often fail to demonstrate it in our life and the world around us! We already have conceived within our mortal mind, that it is not normal for Superman to fly through the air, with jet lightning speed. Take a moment to process this thought. Fictional movies, with all of their brilliant marketing strategies of superheroes, are actually taking from the pages of the Bible.

If you are like me, you probably never thought of it in that particular manner before - the Bible being filled with superheroes. The Bible is filled with all kind of supernatural acts powered by the Spirit of the Lord. Flip throughout the pages of the Bible and you will take a glimpse at men that were clothed with supernatural power and ability from Heaven.

Let's take a quick glance into the life of the last judge of Israel, Samson. Samson was a man with uncommon supernatural strength, that had the ability to tear lions and human militias apart when the Holy Spirit overtook. What enabled this man to be able to accomplish such amazing feats? The Holy Spirit! The Bible informs us that Samson was endowed with power from the Holy Spirit to walk in amazing Olympian strength that had never been seen by a mere human being before on earth.

Another one of the accounts that stands out immediately in my mind is Peter defying the very laws of nature by walking on the sea. If walking on water and tearing a lion to pieces are not acts of the supernatural then I don't know what is, honestly. The water didn't turn into cement nor did the water stop moving. Peter simple took the Lord at his word and stepped outside of the boat and the realm of what seemed humanly possible and began walking on the water of the sea.

The Spirit of the Lord will prompt us to do some extraordinary things that may not make any sense to us at the time. However, He will lead us along a path to break us out of the mundane routine of events or the very construct of what we have become so accustomed to in our life. There have been times when I could notice a parallel to my natural and spiritual life. If I was just going through the motions of work, family obligations, taking out the trash, attending church, etc., it was highly probable that my spiritual life had begun to cool down as well. I have noticed that God will allow a supernatural event to take place to shake you out of the spiritual apathy that can leave you simply going through the motions of ministry, life, and your personal spiritual walk with Him. Can you imagine, how that one experience with the Lord that night, revolutionized not only Peter's life but the other disciples that were in the boat that night as they watched him walk on water to defy every scientific rule under the sun? This must not have only startled them but rekindled their faith in Christ. Even Jesus may have had taken time out to take a picture of this miracle taking place. Jesus is the Son of God but here was a mortal walking on the water in the middle of the sea. What a scene that would have been to capture that rainy night?

CHAPTER 19
The Spirit Gives Us Revelation

I will be the first to admit it. My love of the Holy Spirit grows each and every time He gives me revelation regarding a certain matter. It can be a verse that He shows me during my personal devotional time that convicts or inspires me to change or when He suddenly awakens in the middle of the night with a burden to pray for someone only to find out that person had been battling depression and was contemplating giving up hope in God. God shows me faithfully with time that He is more than able to do all that I ask in the midst of life's unexpected turn of events. The Holy Spirit has been likened to the wind in the Bible. He comes and goes He pleases in and around our circumstances and sometimes without any previous notice of His arrival. So, it's best to always be in expectation for revelation.

A while back, I was waiting at the baggage claim area in a local airport. The Holy Spirit said to me "Spirit of control." You see when this happens to me. I immediately look for people, places, groups, or things around me to identify with that prophetic revelation. I honestly did know what the Holy Spirit was talking about or whom. In a matter of days, it all made perfect sense. Later that day, I was introduced to an individual that was subtle in their manipulation and control of someone I knew at the time.

Revelation from the Spirit of God can come at any time and place, so you must have a willing spiritual ear to expect the Holy Spirit to reveal things suddenly. It could be while sitting in a class at school, shopping at the mall, changing clothes in your bedroom, jogging in the neighborhood park, or even while engaging in activity that is not pleasing to God when suddenly He gives you divine revelation regarding. It doesn't matter the circumstances. If God wants to speak, He will. I once read a memoir of a man who while smoking a cigarette was told by God to leave his business and become a missionary to a specific African nation. Less than a month later, he had his bags packed and was walking on a plane whose destination was across the Atlantic Ocean.

I remember one spring afternoon, I went to check on my mother's apartment while she was out of town visiting family members in Houston, Texas to make sure everything was secure. I had just used the restroom and turned on the faucet to begin to wash my hands when I heard the distinct voice of the Holy Spirit say to me, "Don't trust Elliot." Elliot is not really the guy's name but what I heard in the bathroom confirmed my suspicions of him. When I heard that soft subtle voice of God speaking, I automatically knew who was speaking and the warning He was trying to deliver to me that day. Some lessons from the Holy Spirit come with time and experience. Also, there was no one in the house at the time but me. I can't really say that I was shocked that the Holy Spirit revealed this to me. By this time in my walk with the Lord, I had come to expect that anything is possible when it comes to the way, timing, method, and manner in which God chooses to speak to His children.

So, what do you do when the Holy Spirit tells you not to trust someone? Simple, you don't trust that person! Not even for a second should you think twice about what the Lord speaks to. One of the lessons that I have learned walking with the Holy Spirit is that some revelations are immediately understood and there will be times when it will take months to discern the message from Him. You see, I already had my doubts about Elliot, and I had begun to modestly question the motives and character of this guy. He was a fast talker and a street hustler. From my world, in the inner city, a slick talker is someone that has to be watched very closely. I noticed he was always trying to pull a quick hustle on someone even if he had to take it by force. Even though I knew Elliot since our childhood days, it was quite evident that his familiarity and affiliation with the streets had produced over the years a man who was chasing the quick dollar, most often in an illegal way of sorts. I shared what the Holy Spirit had revealed to me with the young lady that I was dating at the time. I simply let time take it's place.

One afternoon, I was headed to go run an errand and Elliot was walking out of his relative's house with some bags. He explained to me that he just got into an altercation with his relative and that he needed me to drop him and a young lady up the road. I dropped him off and didn't hear from him until two months later when he was arrested on charges of burglary. When the Holy Spirit gives you revelation. Please, take heed!

Growing up as my mother's only child, I loved going to church. My mother made it possible that I was involved in almost every activity and support group a child could participate in at the time in that church. I was a youth usher, junior deacon, choir member, drill team participant, and was active in all of the church plays and functions for the kids throughout the year. I loved going to my church as kid because of the fellowship. Especially, those days when we kids were responsible for ushering. After we were relieved of our duties and the preacher begin to give his sermon, we used to sit in the back of the church, pass notes and candy around until the youth usher director would softly reprimand us to be quiet and pay attention to what the preacher had to say. I was never taught during the early part of my church life and spiritual development that the Lord could reveal things about the intimate details and even sins of someone else's lifestyle supernaturally to us. I guess I was taking all of the other religious courses like the rest of the kids throughout the city during Sunday school and Wednesday night Bible study. We learned about Jonah and the whale but failed to learn how to discern the Spirit's voice.

The Bible states in Daniel 2:47, "The king answered unto Daniel, and said, of a truth it is, that your God is a God of gods, and a Lord of kings, and a revealer of secrets, seeing thou couldest reveal this secret." So, when I heard the words of the Lord that night in the bedroom over a decade ago, while I was sleeping next to a young lady that I had just started dating, it turned my whole world upside down forever. The words I use to sing as a young boy in the youth choir rose up within me later after the revelatory experience from Him resonated in my spirit and heart. The song goes, "Jesus loves me, yes, He does." That night will forever be marked upon the memory of my mind and soul as one of the many turning points in my spiritual life that have helped me to understand the complexity and mysterious ways of an all seeing and loving God.

Up until that night, if you would have asked me, "Does God love me?" I would have replied, "Of course He does, but there may be some things that he is not happy with that I do - but overall, He genuinely loves me." My understanding of the omniscient ways of God soared to a new level months after the event that occurred that particular night. It was a regular Saturday night. I had already hung out with the fellows and gotten something to eat afterwards during the afternoon I decided to visit a new female companion. So, after finishing my meal and watching a little bit of television at her apartment, I decided to spend the night and go to sleep. After we said good night to one another, we both silently drifted off to sleep. Are you ready for what happened next? In the middle of the dark calm night of that sprawling city I heard these words loud and clear, "She's gay!" I immediately jumped up in the bed, sweating profusely and looked all around the room. The only other person in the room with me on that dark city night, was the young lady that I had just started dating. The problem is that she was sound asleep. It was just like the experience the Apostle Paul had along with some other men on the road toward Damascus. The Bible informs us in the Book of Acts 9:7," the men with Saul stood speechless, for they heard the sound of someone's voice but saw no one!" I heard a voice, but I didn't see the person who had spoken those two words. I wasn't frightened but neither was my inner spirit and heart at peace either. What do you do in a situation when a voice reveals to you the secret lifestyle of someone that you didn't know even existed? Do you believe it at all?

I readily accepted that I heard a voice that night without a face. In my heart I knew that voice had spoken to me from the spiritual world. Now I had the long and tedious process of trying to discern whether that was the voice of a demon or the voice of the Holy Spirit. There are certain lessons learned during your walk with the Lord that no one can answer but God. Others can provide a fragment of guidance, counsel, or their very own personal experience but sometimes God decides to wait before He answers your questions. I had never experienced hearing a voice in the dark before in my entire life. Now mind you, I had only been walking with the Lord for a year and a few months, so this was all new to me. This rocked the core of my theological beliefs and personal understanding of who and what God is able to do. I guess the only reasoning for this is because I never knew God would reveal the personal secret lifestyle of someone, I had met only a month before. Like so many of you, I had safely tucked God away in a box.

When it comes to receiving revelation from God, it is always pertinent that you take the matter before Him in prayer from the very beginning. Too many voices from people can bring confusion concerning the matter. So maybe you are thinking what did I do after I heard the heavenly voice that night in the in the bedroom? I simply asked the person who was sleeping next to me if they had anything to tell me. Can you believe that? I was expecting this young lady to reveal her deepest secret to me. I didn't need her to do it because God loved me enough to reveal it for me. Her response was flat-out denial.

One of the lessons that I want to impart unto you in this chapter, is that when the Holy Spirit gives you revelation concerning a certain matter, the first thing you need to do is pray about the revelation and immediately ask the Lord what to do with the information that has been revealed. There was a time when I received prophetic revelation in a dream on how one of the spouses in a marriage was cheating with someone very close to their spouse. Well something like this shouldn't be spoken of to others, especially to either one of the spouses until given direction from the Lord. Some things just need to be taken before the throne of heaven in fervent intercession and fasting.

Whenever His Spirit gives a revelation, we must be willing to be sensitive to the message He is trying to convey to us. We must be willing to muse over the words of the Spirit when He speaks to us because He is a discerner of the thoughts and mind of men. He sees and knows what we don't know or perceive. We need to begin to change our thought process on how we as Christians begin to look at the role of the Holy Spirit in our life on an everyday basis. The churches here in America must place their focus on teaching the masses of followers that we actually have a divine advantage over unbelievers in the world who don't believe in God. What would happen if we started teaching the youth and new believers in Christianity that fill our churches every Sunday morning how to listen for the voice of the Holy Spirit on how to select the correct stocks on Wall Street or allow the Spirit to guide us into the correct career choices? What would happen if we started praying and fasting with our children before they left for college so that the Spirit of the Lord would lead them to the college that God desires for them to attend? The Spirit of God has the providential power to steer His elect to their specific career path and specific calling for their lives that God preordained before the foundations of the world for His own.

Some of us have wasted so much time trying to follow our own plans that unfortunately amounts to years and for some, decades because we have been out of the will of God for such an extensive time. Many pursue the path that the Lord never wanted for our life in the first place. We must begin to change our mindsets about being willing and submissive to receive the revelation of the Holy Spirit. Let our plans be the very blueprints that He wrote in eternity for us before we were a thought conceived in the minds of our parents. We find His revelation in prayer and waiting silently at His feet. Let us not follow the pattern of His people in Psalm 106:13, for it states that "they wouldn't wait for his counsel." The revelation of the Holy Spirit is His divine counsel.

In conclusion, the Holy Spirit has a pattern usually to

reveal to us what is going on around us unexpectedly. Whether it's family members, things in our communities, or future events that will take place in the nations abroad, we must have a willing heart to receive the revelations of the Holy Spirit.

CHAPTER 20
Developing A Relationship With The Holy Spirit

One of the greatest discoveries I have made in my walk with God is the ability to recognize and cultivate my relationship with the Holy Spirit. It took time because I was still trying to tune in to how the Lord would communicate to me. It seemed to me sometimes as soon I figured out one way in which God would communicate to me, He would switch it up to keep me on my toes spiritually. I've always had a heart to know God on a personal basis. So, for me, from the very beginning of my relationship with the Lord it was always obvious that it was going to take time and sacrifice to develop a closeness with God. So far, I have explained in simplicity some of the lessons that the Holy Spirit has revealed to me over the last decade and plus years.

What are you willing to do to grow closer in your

relationship with the Holy Spirit? God is just waiting to bring you closer to Him by His Spirit. Have you ever been in a relationship with a person and found yourself so infatuated with this person that stayed up all night talking on the phone? Before you even brush your teeth in the morning, you're already sending an email or a text message to your church. Why does this occur so many times in the beginning of relationships to people we really like? It is because that person has captured your attention and you find yourself attracted to this individual. This drives you not only to find out as much as you can about that person but to spend time with them a well. The more you spend time with that person whether hanging out at the local coffee shop watching movies together or the sofa, or just taking a walk in the park, you begin to learn more about them, their fears, flaws, strengths, and even insecurities. This is the exact same way God wants us to wholeheartedly pursue a relationship with the Holy Spirit. The more time spent laying prostrate and sitting in silence in anticipation for direction or to HEAR His voice, the more captivated we will become with the personality of who and what the Holy Spirit is personally to you.

Fasting is one of those spiritual disciplines that over the last few years has been rekindled among the churches in America to a certain extent. I don't remember how I learned about fasting. I'm sure one of the brothers on the campus of Morehouse college who was an experienced Christian shared with me about the dynamic potential wrapped up in this spiritual exercise. After I became saved in the spring of 2001, I automatically went on a Daniel fast for about a week or so. I felt so close to the Lord. Every time I opened my bible to search the scriptures or drop to my knees in prayer, the sweet presence of the Holy Spirit descended upon my entire being. I felt so close to God. As I'm typing this chapter, I've begun a fast in obedience to the prompting of the Holy Spirit. Whenever the Lord calls us to fast, we should obey. Fasting is no easy exercise in the very beginning stages. However, the sacrifice is well worth it. Fasting can be done in a variety of ways. Even though some believe a fast can be considered abstaining from things such as watching television or participating in social media for an extended set of time. I'm not against these form of fasts at all because when you decide to fast you should aside as much time as possible to place yourself in a position to hear from God and allow him to minister to you. So, having the least distractions possible is the best way to approach a fast. But a true fast can be taken straight from the pages of the Bible. Moses is one of the greatest examples of a person who fasted found in the Old Testament. He fasted without water and food of any type while on the mountain of Sinai for exactly for forty days. Now I've never gone on an extended fast for up to forty days as yet. The most I've fasted on one occasion has been thirteen days of nothing but liquids. This 40 day fast of Moses was supernatural (Exodus 34:28).

Another popular fast is the Daniel fast in which you

fast from meat and bread for up to twenty-one days eating nothing but fruits, vegetables, and drinking water. Altering the fast to suit your body needs should always be taken into careful prayer and consideration. Usually when I fast, I like to just drink coffee, Gatorade, or just water. Sometimes I may just drink water during the day and a cup of coffee at nighttime. When it comes to fasting, you must allow the Lord to lead you. Fasting will allow you to draw closer to God in ways you have never dreamed of. While the first few days can be a very difficult adjustment, this is the time to draw on the strength of the Lord and the power of the Holy Spirit. It places you in a unique position to rely more on God and less on yourself. The more your flesh is weakened through the fasting, the more that you will find that the Spirit of the Lord is willing to step in to assist you in the process of drawing closer to him. This is the whole point in fasting. To draw closer unto God. ("Draw nigh to God and He will draw nigh to you." James 4:8)

My experiences with fasting have always been consistent. Fasting will bring out the worst and the best that rests on the inside of you. You will find yourself tapping into power that you never knew existed on the inside of your spirit. Your sense of spiritual discernment will be sharpened. Your ability to discern the voice of the spirit will be keener and your prayers will be bolder and more effective. You will have more peace and your faith will begin to rise to another level. You will find that your sensitivity will heighten, and your awareness of Spirit of the Lord will be more present than ever before. On the other hand, when you are walking out the steps of a fast as you pray and seek the face of God in your prayer closet, the Lord will begin to deal with you about sins, attitudes, and relationships that need to be mended. You will experience yourself reading the bible and the Lord convicting you of things that you may never have known existed in your life. Fasting makes us come face to face with our weaknesses and secret sins that we have intentionally not dealt with in our own lives.

As I am writing this chapter, the Holy Spirit is reminding me of the story of the man who had a son that was possessed by demons. The gospels inform us that the deans caused the boy to be deaf, blind, and epileptic. There demonic assignment was successful in the young boy's life. They were on the verge of killing him. Killing him physically would have destroyed not only his future and the plan of God for his life, but emotionally destroyed his father as well. The father was either a believer in Christ or he was privy to the accounts of the miracle working power of Jesus of Nazareth. Either way, the man had enough humility, urgency, and common sense to seek the headquarters of Jesus evangelistic ministry. On arrival to the headquarters, the father found out that Jesus is nowhere to be found. ...Probably somewhere praying or ministering to the sick. Whatever the case may have been, due to the temporary absence of Jesus at the time, He approached the disciples of Jesus asking for their spiritual diagnosis and assistance. (Matthew 17:14-20). After attempting to cast out the demons from the young child, not once and numerous times. The disciples cannot, nether can those around them, nor the father cast out these demons. According to divine timing, Jesus comes back to the campgrounds to overhear and witness the failed exorcism taking place. These words of Jesus revolutionized my life. "Some things only come out by fasting and prayer. " As you fast and pray draw closer to the power of the Holy Spirit. You will find yourself discerning things in your life that you have dealt with come to the surface. Regret. Anger. Lust. Lack of faith. Stubbornness. Pride. Rebellion. Allow God to not only bring these things to the surface but allow the Holy Spirit to remove these hindrances from your life. It will not be easy. It will even be painful in some instances. But if you truly desire for your relationship with the Holy Spirit to be more intimate and effective, then you must deal with the toxic issues and hindrances that are keeping you and Him from a deeper, closer walk (Isaiah 58:6). It was not a coincidence that Paul wrote to the church in Ephesians 4:30, "do not grieve the holy spirit". The things in your life that grieve or mourn the Holy Spirit are what is keeping you from a more fruitful walk with Him. Allow the process of fasting to purge you of these things that you do not have the power to break with your own power and will.

Confession is another one of things that will bring you

deeper into the things of the Spirit. The Bible admonishes us to "confess our sins one to another". I remember during my last year of college a was part of a Christian youth fellowship organization on campus. A few of the members and myself would pile into my two door Honda civic and drive a few blocks to the campus of the Interdenominational Theological Center. One of the Christian youth fellowship attended the seminary and for nearly three weeks we would lay prostrate and seek the face of God with our whole hearts. I will never forget the move of God during those three weeks. Before we would pray, we see how each other was doing personally and how classes were going. Then we would go around in a circle and confess our sins to one another. I'm talking about this was the most transparent I've ever been with Christians before in my life. There was no judging nor condemnation. People revealed some of their most deep and conflicted sins. These young folks would confess of being in bondage to masturbation, pornography, hearts filled of lust, and lack of trust in the provision of God. We would pray for one another and then immediately find a corner to lay prostrate to seek the face of the Lord. I tell you! There was such a move of God that people would weep while lying on their face. Others would cry out to the Lord while walking around in that small campus apartment. There was no pride or masks. All of our struggles and sins were laid before one another and God.

In our desperate response to get right with Him. God

gave us an outpouring of His spirit. This was the only time where I felt like I was living what Joel prophesied about in Joel 2:28, " in the last days, God says, I will pour out My Spirit on all people. Your sons and daughters will prophesy, your young men will see visions, your old men will dream dreams." We would enter that apartment around eight at night and leave sometimes at two in the morning. After much travailing, confessions of sins, intercession, ministering to one another, and gut-wrenching prayer, we would always end the prayer session in silence for at least ten to fifteen minutes just soaking in the presence of God.

I remember walking out of the apartment just feeling the weight of the Glory of God upon my shoulders. There were times when I was driving back to my dorm room and I wouldn't be able to go to sleep because of the tangible presence of the Holy Spirit. I've yet to experience a move of God among my peers in the Christian faith or in any church that I've attended besides the spoken word at Holy Tabernacle in Fort Worth, Texas led by pastor Matthew Brown. Even then, no prayer meeting or intercession of the saints that I've gathered among to seek God's hand has ever matched up to this level of intimacy with the Holy Spirit. Why is this so? Because everyone that attended these meetings were humble enough to repent and confess their sins and admit their need of God. All pride was laid at the altar nightly for nearly three weeks. I thirst and hunger for this type of move of God. Confession of your sins will bring a move of the Holy Spirit like you have never experienced before!

CONCLUSION

Words can't explain the journey that I have experienced with the Holy Spirit. It's still a learning process. God has shown that He is truly a provider in all areas. We should always depend on the Holy Spirit should on a daily basis. There will be times when you make decisions without His wise counsel or even make decisions that are against His will. The key to learning lessons from the Holy Spirit is to remain humble and always have an open ear and discerning eye to determine when He is trying to speak to you. It will not always be in a whisper. Sometimes He will speak through a spouse or a radio broadcast. Honestly, His Spirit is always trying to communicate to each one of us in spite of our situation at the current moment. These lessons that I have shared with you in this book took over a decade for me to learn. For you, the lessons that are shared in the book can assist you in your walk with God and if you use them, you can shorten your learning curve. God loves each one of us and desires for us to run this race with diligence and patience. I learned these lessons while unemployed, frustrated with the turn of events of my life, and at times when all was going well. His greatest presentations of these lessons came a day at a time, usually when I least expected it. Continue to walk humbly with our God and know that there is a greater dimension of His riches in store for you on this side of Heaven.

Respectfully His Evangelist,
Patrick Hackett-Kemp

AUTHOR BIO

An evangelist of the Gospel for over sixteen years, Patrick Hackett-Kemp has served in many capacities to include a short stint as an inner city pastor. He is fluent in his giftings and endowments from the Holy Spirit operating frequently in the Word of knowledge, gifts of healing, prophecy, administration, and the discernment of spirits. He has preached in prisons, conferences, churches, revivals, conducted Bible studies, and even ministered on street corners from California to Georgia. His greatest desire is to become more committed to a life of consecrated prayer and to eventually serve as a missionary to Thailand. He resides in Texas, along with his wife Kayla, and has been blessed with six children.

www.ingramcontent.com/pod-product-compliance
Lightning Source LLC
Chambersburg PA
CBHW031359040426
42444CB00005B/350